George Gordon Byron, Harutiwn Awgerean

A Grammer

Armenian and English

George Gordon Byron, Harutiwn Awgerean

A Grammer
Armenian and English

ISBN/EAN: 9783337287924

Printed in Europe, USA, Canada, Australia, Japan

Cover: Foto ©Andreas Hilbeck / pixelio.de

More available books at **www.hansebooks.com**

GRAMMAR

—

Grammar teaches the art of speaking and writing correctly.

Human discourse is formed of letters, syllables and words.

Letters are the elements of a syllable.

A syllable is either one letter, or the union of letters.

A word is one or more syllables, which express some thing.

The union of words to explain our thoughts completely is called discourse.

The harmony of words with the rules of Grammar is called Syntax.

ALPHABET

The Armenian Alphabet consists of thirty - eight letters

PRINTING		NAME	SOUND	READING
Ա	ա	ipe	a as in part.	Ատոր ātór chair.
Բ	բ	pēn	p soft.	Բերան pērán mouth.
Գ	գ	kim	k, q.	Գառն karn lamb.
Դ	դ	tā	t soft.	Դուռն toorn door.
Ե	ե	yēlch	ye as in yes.	Երգ yerk song.
Զ	զ	zā	z or s between two vowels.	Զոր zor army
Է	է	ē	e as in met.	Էագ ēag being.
Ը	ը	yet	e as in her, or like the french e mute in the monosyllables me, ne, ce.	Ընկեր ungḡēr companion.
Թ	թ	toe	t hard.	Թիվ tiv number.
Ժ	ժ	zhē	j french, or s in pleasure and z in azure.	Ժամ zham hour.

				Pronunciation	Example		Meaning
←	←	←	ceni	i short or e as in *he, be*.	*eemūsd*	եմաստ	meaning.
←	←	←	leun	l as in *lunatic*.	*luis*	լոյս	light.
←	←	←	khē	kh as greek χ, or german *ch*.	*khāvār*	խաւար	dark.
←	←	←	dzā	dz or cz in *czar*, or z in *mezzotinto*.	*dzār*	ծառ	tree.
←	←	←	ghen	g hard as *good*.	*gātn*	գաղն	milk.
←	←	←	hoe	h.	*hyer*	հեր	hair.
←	←	←	tzā	tz soft.	*tzine*	ձայն	voice.
←	←	←	ghād	gh as new greek γ, or parisian *r*.	*gheg*	ղեկ	rodder.
←	←	←	jē	j or dg *judge*.	*jar*	ճառ	discourse.
←	←	←	man	m.	*mire*	մայր	mother.
←	←	←	he	h soft in beginning of words; y as *boy* in the midst; and mute at the end.	*hart*	յարդ	straw.
←	←	←	noo	n.	*nāmāg*	նամակ	letter.
←	←	←	shū	sh.	*shoon*	շուն	dog.
←	←	←	wo	wo as in *word*.	*worty*	որդի	son.
←	←	←	tchā	tch or ch in *fetch* and *such*.	*tchămich*	չամիչ	raisin.
←	←	←	bē	b.	*bānir*	բանիր	cheese.
←	←	←	tshē	tsh or ch soft as in *church*, or like *t* in *nature*.	*tshur*	տշուր	water.
←	←	←	rā	r hard.	*roomp*	ռումբ	bomb.

PRINTING	NAME	SOUND	READING
	sē	s.	Սուրբ soorp saint.
	vēv	v.	Վարդ vārt rose.
	deune	d.	Sէր dēr sir.
	rē	r soft.	Ռամ rām flock.
	tzo	tz hard.	Ցուլ tzul bull.
	une or hune	u long as in mute, or w in vowel.	Իւն une poisin.
	pure	p.	Փունջ poonch bunch.
	kē	k hard or ch as in chaos.	Քար kar stone.
	o	o.	Օդ ot air.
	fē	f or ph.	Ֆարդ fārd odd.

N. B. ā marked with a long accent is pronounced like *a* in French, and ē like *e* in Italian. The sounds given here are the nearest that can be given in English characters: but in some cases the master's voice is indispensable to convey a clear idea of the pronunciation.

The 36 Characters from Ս to Ք were formed in the fourth century, the last two Օ and Ֆ were introduced into the Armenian Alphabet in the twelfth century.

EXAMPLE OF READING

THE LORD'S PRAYER

Հայր մեր որ յերկինս, սուրբ եղիցի
Hāyr myer wor hyergins, soorp . yeghitzi

անուն քո. եկեսցէ արքայութիւն քո.
ānoon . ko; yegestzē ārkāyootune ko;

եղիցին կամք քո որպէս յերկինս եւ յերկ-
yeghitzin gamk ko worbēs hyergins yev hyerg-

րի. Զհաց մեր հանապազորդ տուր մեզ
ri. Ezhātz myer hānābāzort door mez

այսօր։ Եւ թող մեզ զպարտիս մեր, որպէս
āyssor; yev togh myez ezbardis ınyer, worbēs

եւ մեք թողումք մերոց պարտապանաց. եւ
yēv myek toghoomk myerotz bārdābānatz; yev

մի տանիր զմեզ ՚ի փորձութիւն, այլ փրկեա՛
mi dānir ezmyez i portzootune, āyl pergiā

զմեզ ի չարէն։ Զի քո է ար-
ezmyez i tchārēn. Zi ko ē ar-

քայութիւն եւ զօրութիւն եւ փառք յաւիտեանս
kāyootune yev zorootune yev pārk hāvidyāns.

ամէն։
amēn.

Vowels

ա, ե, է, ը, ի, ո, ւ, օ.

Consonants

բ, գ, դ, զ, թ, ժ, լ, խ, ծ, կ, հ, ձ, ղ,
ճ, մ, յ, ն, շ, չ, պ, ջ, ռ, ս, վ, տ, ր,
ց, փ, ք, ֆ.

SYLLABLE

A syllable is an articulate sound, as, առ,
ar. նա, na. դար, tar. աղդ, aghd. որմ,
worm. բարդ, part. գառն, karn. դեմք, temk.
զոր, zor. ընդ, unt. թիւ, tiv, ժամ, zham,
լոյս, looyce, ծառ, dzar. կալ, gal, Հայր,
hire. ծային, tzine. ճառ, jar. միր, mire. շուն,
shoon. չար, tchar. ջուր, tshoor or chiure.
սուրբ, soorp. տեր, der. րամ, ram. ցու,
tzoo. ւիւթ, ute or ewt. փարք, park.

A syllable may be also composed of six
letters, as սեամբք, siampk. ջուրբք, chiurpk.

Two or three consonants are sometimes
formed before or after a vowel.

Double consonants at the end of a syllable
are pronounced short, as, տարր, darr, ցաղ
դացք, caghack.

When the word ends with double ն, in
the pronunciation an ը is inserted, as,
մատնն (մատնըն) madnun. ձեռնն (ձեռնըն)
tziernun.

So also when in the beginning of a word the same consonant is doubled, as, շշուկ (շըշուկ) *shushoog*. կկոց (կըկոց) *gugotz*.

When the liquids ն, ղ, ր, are at the end of a syllable after another consonant, they have equally in the pronunciation the letter ը, as, մուկն (մուկըն) *moogun*. աստղ (աս֊տըղ) *asdugh*. դուստր (դուստըր) *toosder*.

But not when they precede the consonant, as, կունդ, *coond*. աղդ, *aghd*. կարկ, *gark*.

Likewise when the consonants are different, as, թուղթ, *tooght*. սուրբք, *soorpk*. հողմք, *hoghmk*.

In the beginning of many words between two consonants the letter ը is understood in the oblique cases instead of another vowel of the nominative case, as, ծուկն, *tzoogun*. ծկան (ծըկան) *tzugan*. մշդ, *mishd*. մշտակայ (մըշտակայ) *mushdaga*.

FAMILIAR ABBREVIATIONS

ամ	ամենայն.	թէ or է	թէեն է.
յն	այսինքն.	թբ or բ	թեամբ.
ած	Աստուած.	ի վր	ի վերայ.
այ	Աստուծոյ.	կմ	կամ.
ավ	Աստուծով.	Յս	Յիսուս.
բզմ	բազում.	նր	նորա.
դր	դորա.	նմնէ	նմանէ.
եղ	եալ.	նք	նորա.
և	եւ.	նյ	նոցա.
նա	և այն.	նս	նոսա.

1*

Ը	ընդ.	ուն	որպէս.
Ը	բստ.	ւս or ֆ	պէս.
Թ̄ or Ժ	Թիւն.	՞ր	սորա.
ԹԷ or Ժ	Թեան.	՞մէ	սմանէ.
մբ	սթա.	ւ՞ո	վան.
մյ	սցա.	ւ՞յ	վան որոյ.
մյէ	սցանէ.	՞ր	տէր.
՞ր	սուրբ.	՞ս	տեառն.
մէյ	սրբոյ.	Է̄	քան.
մէց	սրբոց.	Քն	Քրիստոս ։

WORD

A word is an articulate sound expressive of our ideas.

Words in the Armenian language consist of eight parts of speech; Nouns, Pronouns, Verbs, Participles, Prepositions, Adverbs, Conjunctions, Interjections.

NOUN

A noun signifies some substance, or quality, as, մարդ, man. երկիր, earth. լոյս, light. արքայութիւն, kingdom. Հոգի, soul, spirit. անձն, person. բնութիւն, nature. միտք, mind, thought. բարի, good. գեղեցիկ, handsome. քաղցր, sweet. մեծ, great.

In nouns six peculiarities are to be considered: Gender, Form, Species or Kind, Number, Case, Declension.

GENDER

In the Armenian language the genders are distinguished by their natural significations, as

MASCULINE

Ադամ, *Adam.* Մովսէս, *Moses.* Պետրոս, *Peter.* Գրիգոր, *Gregory.* Վարդան, *Vardan,* etc.

Հայր, *father.* Եղբայր, *brother.* ուսոր, *son, a male-child.* փեսայ, *a husband, spouse.* աներ, *a father-in-law.* քեռի, *uncle, a mother's brother.* կնքահայր, *gossip, Godfather.* այր, *man, husband.* ծառայ, *a man-servant.* Թագաւոր *or* արքայ, *king.* նախարար, *satrap, a peer.* ցուլ, *a bull.* եզն, *an ox.* քաղ, *a he-goat.* խոյ, *ram, a male sheep.* զուարակ, *bullock, a young ox.* եղջերու, *a stag.* արագաղ, *cock,* etc.

Ատեան, *tribunal.* զօր, *soldiers.* հեծելագունդ, *cavalry, horse-troops,* etc.

FEMININE

Եւայ, *Eve.* Սառա, *Sarah.* Մարիամ, *Mary.* Շուշան *or* Շուշանիկ, *Susanna.* Վարդուհի, *Rose,* etc.

Հանի, *grandmother.* մայր, *mother.* քոյր, *sister.* հարսն, *spouse, bride.* կին, *woman; wife.* դուստր, *daughter.* աղջիկ, *girl, maid.* զոքանչ, *mother-in-law.* նու, *son's wife, daughter-in-law.* սկեսուր, *mother-in-law,*

12

husband's mother. Կնքամայր, gossip, God-
mother. դշխոյ, տիկին, թագուհի., queen,
princess. օրիորդ, young girl. նաժիշտ,
աղախին, servant-maid. կով, cow. երինջ,
heifer, a young cow. մաքի, ewe, female
sheep. մարի, hen. եղն, hind, etc.

Մարդ, man. որդի, զաւակ, child. տղայ,
infant. ժառանգ, an heir. թոռն, grandson,
or grand-daughter. թռչուն, bird. առիւծ,
lion, or lioness. կորիւն, a young beast. ձագ,
chick, chicken. հաւ, bird, fowl. ոչխար,
sheep. արջառ, cattle. աղաւնի, pigeon, dove.
ձի, horse. շուն, dog, bitch. դիւթ, charmer.
մարգարէ, prophet, or prophetess, etc.

Ջուր, water. օդ, air. հող, earth. մար-
մին, body. երկինք, heaven. լոյս, light.
ծառ, tree. ձեռք, hand. ոտք, foot. հոգի,
soul, spirit. միտք, mind. տուն, house. ա-
թոռ, chair. կեանք, life. մահ, death. համ-
բերութիւն, patience. անիրաւութիւն, in-
justice, etc.

The genders are distinguished also in
this manner: Այր մարգարէ, prophet, a
male prophet. կին մարգարէ, prophetess, a
female prophet. այր մարդ, man, male. կին
մարդ, woman. մատակ առիւծ, lioness, fe-

male lion, a she-lion. արու աղաւնի, *male pigeon.* աղջիկ, աղայ, *girl, a female child,* etc.

Some genders are indicated also by their terminations, as

MASCULINE

Յովհաննէս, *John.* Յուլիանոս, *Julian.* Աթանասիոս, *Athanasius.* Թէոդորոս, *Theodore,* etc.

FEMININE

Յովհաննա, *Joan.* Յուլիանէ, *Juliana.* Աթանասիա, *Athanasia.* Թէոդորա, *Theodora,* etc.

Վարդուհի, *Rose.* քրմուհի, *a priestess heathenish.* քահանայուհի, *a priestess.* մարգարէուհի, *a prophetess.* Աստուածուհի, *Goddess.* արքայուհի, թագուհի, տիկրուհի, *queen, princess.* վկայուհի, *a she-martyr.* Աբբատուհի, *an Abbess.* Սարկաւագուհի, *Deaconess,* etc.

Վարդանոյշ, *Vard's daughter.* Սահականոյշ, *Isaac's daughter.* Խոսրովիդուխտ, *Chosroes' daughter.* Որմզդուխտ, *Hormistus' daughter,* etc.

FORM

The forms of the nouns are three: simple, as, մարդ, *man:* Accompanied by a particle before, as, անմարդ, *inhuman:* Composed of entire words, as, մարդասէր, *human, kind.*

The different modes of producing compound epithets and words, are the treasure and ornament of the Armenian language; a thousand varieties of compounded words may be made in this tongue as may be perceived in the Armenian grammar published 1815.

SPECIES or KIND

There are two kinds of words: Primitive, as, *մարդ*, *man:* and Derivative or Derived having at the termination a particle, as, *մարդկային*, *human.*

The Derivatives are most abundant in the Armenian language.

NUMBER

Numbers are two: Singular, as, *մարդ*, *man:* and Plural, as, *մարդք* or *մարդիկ*, *men.*

The plural of some nouns is formed in a particular manner, as, *կին*, *woman*, *կանայք*, *women.* *վանք*, *convent*, *վանորայք*, *վանորեայք* or *վաներայք*, *convents.* *գիր* or *գիրք*, *book*, *գրեան*, *books.* *մանուկ*, *child*, *boy*, *մանկտի*, *children*, *boys.*

The proper nouns are sometimes made plural with the particle *եանք*, as, *Գրիգոր*, *Gregory*, *Գրիգորեանք*, *Gregories.* *Յոհաննէս*, *John*, *Յոհաննիւեանք*, *Johns.*

The cases in the Armenian language according to the modern authors are *ten* in number.

1. Nominative, *Մարդ*, *the man.*
2. Genitive, *Մարդոյ*, *of the man.*
3. Dative, *Մարդոյ* or *'ի Մարդ*, *to the man.*
4. Accusative, *զՄարդ*, *the man.*
5. Ablative, *'ի Մարդոյ*, *from the man.*
6. Narrative, *զՄարդոյ*, *concerning the man.*
7. Instrumental, *Մարդով*, *by means of man.*
8. Circumdative, *զՄարդով*, *about the man.*
9. Commorative, *'ի Մարդ* or *'ի Մարդում*; *in the man.*
10. Vocative, *ով Մարդ*, *o man!*

It is to be remarked in this declension that the second case is changed in the termination. The third in the termination, and is then denominated the *dative-declined-in the-termination:* and sometimes has before it a letter or preposition, and is then called the *dative-with-the-preposition.* The fourth case has before it the letter զ, which is sometimes omitted or understood. The fifth case changes in the termination, and has the letter or preposition *'ի* before it; or the letter յ when followed by a vowel. The sixth case likewise changes in the termination, and has before it the letter զ. The seventh case changes in the termination. The eighth case also, and has before it the letter զ.

The ninth case has before it the letters 'ȶ or ȷ, and when changed in the termination has always before it the same letter or preposition. The tenth case has before it the interjection ᴧ or ᴧ, but not always expressed.

According to the ancient authors the cases are properly only six.

1. Nominative.
2. Genitive.
3. Dative.
4. Accusative.
5. Ablative.
6. Instrumental.

And these will be followed in the present grammar.

DECLENSION

Concerning the number of declensions of the nouns the opinions of authors are various: we will reckon *ten* dividing them into two classes according to the grammar published in 1815.

The first class contains six *simple* or *regular* declensions, and the second four *mixed* or *irregular* declensions: and they are distinguished from the second and sixth cases in this manner.

REGULAR DECLENSIONS

	SINGULAR		PLURAL	
	Gen.	*Instr.*	*Gen.*	*Instr.*
1.	ի,	իւ.	ից,	իւք.
2.	ի,	աւ.	աց,	աւք or օք.
3.	ոյ, ւ	ով.	ոց,	ովք.
4.	ան, օր	ամբ.	անց,	ամբք.
5.	ու,	ու.	ուց,	ուք.
6.	եր, եց or	երք or	երց,	երրք or
	եղ,	եղ.	եղց,	եղւք.

IRREGULAR DECLENSIONS

	SINGULAR		PLURAL	
	Gen.	*Instr.*	*Gen.*	*Instr.*
1.	ոյ,	ով or	եաց,	ովք or
		եաւ.	եայց, եաւք or եօք.	
2.	ին,	ամբ.	անց,	ամբք.
3.	ոջ,	աւ or ամբ.	անց,	ամբք.
4.	այ or եայ, աւ or եաւ.			

FIRST DECLENSION

SINGULAR

1. Արքայ, the king.
2. Արքայի, of the king.
3. Արքայի, or Յարքայ յարքայ, to the king.
4. զԱրքայ, the king.

18

5. ⟨Արքայէ⟩, from the king.
6. ⟨Արքայիւ⟩, with or by the king.

PLURAL

1. ⟨Արքայք⟩, the kings.
2. ⟨Արքայից⟩, of the kings.
3. ⟨Արքայից⟩ or ⟨յարքայս⟩, ⟨ցարքայս⟩, to the kings.
4. ⟨զԱրքայս⟩, the kings.
5. ⟨յԱրքայից⟩, from the kings.
6. ⟨Արքայիւք⟩, with or by the kings.

It may be seen by this example that the letters *, *, *, form the plural; but are not always signs of the plural in the termination of a word, as, ⟨քաղաք⟩, city. ⟨լոյս⟩, light. ⟨հաց⟩, bread: which in the plural form ⟨քաղաքք⟩, cities. ⟨լոյսք⟩, the lights. ⟨հացք⟩, the loaves.

The third and fifth cases carry before them the letter *, when the noun begins with a vowel, and the letter '*, when the noun begins with a consonant.

The cases are generally formed either by the addition of a vowel to the nominative, as, ⟨բառ⟩, word, ⟨բառի⟩, of the word, ⟨գետ⟩, river, ⟨գետոյ⟩, of the river. ⟨զգեստ⟩, coat, ⟨զգեստու⟩, of the coat. ⟨Տրդատ⟩, Tiridates, ⟨Տրդատայ⟩, of Tiridates: or by placing in the termination of a word the vowel of the last syllable, as, ⟨դարբին⟩, forger, ⟨դարբնի⟩, of the forger: or by omitting a vowel of the last syllable, as, ⟨ատեան⟩, tribunal, ⟨ատենի⟩, of the tribunal: or by exchanging one

vowel for another, as, պարտէզ, *garden,*
պարտիզի, *of the garden.*

Some nouns have no singular, as, փառք,
glory. բարք, *custom.* դժոխք, *hell.* կուռք,
idol. կեանք, *life,* երեսք, *face.* աղօթք,
prayer, etc.

And others no plural, as, յոյս, *hope.* սէր,
affection, love. քուն, *sleep.* երկիր, *earth,*
ասր, *wool.* խաւար, *the dark,* etc.

SECOND DECLENSION

SINGULAR

1. կարգ, the order.
2. կարգի, of the order.
3. կարգի or 'ի կարգ, առ կարգ, to the order.
4. զկարգ, the order.
5. 'ի կարգէ, from the order.
6. կարգաւ, with *or* by the order.

PLURAL

1. կարգք, the orders.
2. կարգաց, of the orders.
3. կարգաց or 'ի կարգս, to the orders.
4. զկարգս, the orders.
5. 'ի կարգաց, from the orders.
6. կարգաւք or կարգօք, with *or* by the orders.

THIRD DECLENSION

SINGULAR

1. Մարդ, the man.
2. Մարդոյ, of the man.
3. Մարդոյ or մարդում or 'ի մարդ, to the man.
4. զՄարդ, the man.
5. 'ի Մարդոյ, from the man.
6. Մարդով, with *or* by the man.

PLURAL

1. Մարդք, the men.
2. Մարդոց, of the men.
3. Մարդոց or 'ի մարդս, to the men.
4. զՄարդս, the men.
5. 'ի Մարդոց, from the men.
6. Մարդովք, with *or* by the men.

FOURTH DECLENSION

SINGULAR

1. Հիմն, the foundation.
2. Հիման, of the foundation.
3. Հիման or 'ի Հիմն, to the foundation.
4. զՀիմն, the foundation.
5. 'ի Հիմանէ, from the foundation.
6. Հիմամբ, with *or* by the foundation.

PLURAL

1. Հիմունք, the foundations.
2. Հիմանց, of the foundations.

3. Հիմանց or 'ի Հիմունս, to the foundations.
4. զՀիմունս, the foundations.
5. 'ի Հիմանց, from the foundations.
6. Հիմամբք, with or by the foundations.

FIFTH DECLENSION

SINGULAR

1. Գանձ, the treasure.
2. Գանձու, of the treasure.
3. Գանձու or 'ի գանձ, to the treasure.
4. զԳանձ, the treasure.
5. 'ի Գանձէ, from the treasure.
6. Գանձու, with or by the treasure.

PLURAL

1. Գանձք, the treasures.
2. Գանձուց, of the treasures.
3. Գանձուց or 'ի գանձս, to the treasures.
4. զԳանձս, the treasures.
5. 'ի Գանձուց, from the treasures.
6. Գանձուք, with or by the treasures.

SIXTH DECLENSION

SINGULAR

1. Աղբիւր, the fountain.
2. Աղբեր, of the fountain.
3. Աղբեր or յաղբիւր, to the fountain.
4. զԱղբիւր, the fountain.

22

5. *ՅԱղբերէ* or *յաղբիւրէ*, from the fountain.

6. *Աղբերբ* or *աղբերաւ*, with or by the fountain.

1. *Աղբերբ* or *աղբիւրբ*, the fountains.

2. *Աղբերց* or *աղբերաց*, of the fountains.

3. *Աղբերց, աղբերաց* or *յաղբերս, յաղբիւրս*, to the fountains.

4. *զԱղբերս* or *զաղբիւրս*, the fountains.

5. *յԱղբերց* or *յաղբերաց*, from the fountains.

6. *Աղբերբք* or *աղբերաւք*, with *or* by the fountains.

SEVENTH DECLENSION

1. *Տեղի*, the place.

2. *Տեղւոյ*, of the place.

3. *Տեղւոյ* or *տեղւոջ* or *՚ի տեղի*, to the place.

4. *զՏեղի*, the place.

5. *՚ի Տեղւոյ* or *՚ի տեղւոջէ*, from the place.

6. *Տեղեաւ*, with *or* by the place.

1. *Տեղիք*, the places.

2. *Տեղեաց*, of the places.

3. *Տեղեաց* or *՚ի տեղիս*, to the places.

4. *զՏեղիս*, the places.

5. 'ի Տեղեաց, from the places.
6. Տեղեաւք or տեղեօք, with *or* by the places.

EIGHTH DECLENSION

SINGULAR

1. բեռն, the burden.
2. բեռին, of the burden.
3. բեռին or 'ի բեռն, to the burden.
4. զբեռն, the burden.
5. 'ի բեռանէ, from the burden.
6. բեռամբ, with *or* by the burden.

PLURAL

1. բեռինք, the burdens.
2. բեռանց, of the burdens.
3. բեռանց or 'ի բեռինս, to the burdens.
4. զբեռինս, the burdens.
5. 'ի բեռանց, from the burdens.
6. բեռամբք, with *or* by the burdens.

NINTH DECLENSION

SINGULAR

1. կին, the woman *or* the wife.
2. կնոջ, of the woman.
3. կնոջ or 'ի կին, to the woman.
4. զկին, the woman.
5. 'ի կնոջէ, from the woman.
6. կնաւ or կանամբ, with *or* by the woman.

1. կանայք, the women *or* the wives.
2. կանանց, of the women.
3. կանանց or առ կանայս, to the women.
4. զկանայս, the women.
5. 'ի կանանց, from the women.
6. կանամբք, with *or* by the women.

The following are declined in this manner.

SINGULAR

1. Գիւղ or գեօղ, the village.
2. Գեղջ, of the village.
3. Գեղջ or 'ի գիւղ, to the village.
4. զԳիւղ, the village.
5. 'ի Գեղջէ, from the village.
6. Գիւղիւ, with *or* by the village.

PLURAL

1. Գիւղք, the villages.
2. Գիւղից, of the villages.
3. Գիւղից or 'ի գիւղս, to the villages.
4. զԳիւղս, the villages.
5. 'ի Գիւղից, from the villages.
6. Գիւղիւք or գիւղօք, with *or* by the
villages.

SINGULAR

1. Տէր, the Lord, the Master.
2. Տեառն, of the lord.
3. Տեառն or տութր, to the lord.

25

4. * զՏէր*, the lord.
5. *'ի Տեառնէ* or *'ի Տեռնէ*, from the lord.
6. *Տերամբ*, with *or* by the lord.

PLURAL

1. *Տեարք*, the Lords, the Masters.
2. *Տեարց* or *տերանց*, of the lords.
3. *Տեարց*, *տերանց* or *ցտեարս*, to the lords.
4. *զՏեարս*, the lords.
5. *'ի Տեարց* or *'ի տերանց*, from the lords.
6. *Տերամբք*, with *or* by the lords.

SINGULAR

1. *Աւր* or *օր*, the day.
2. *Աւուր*, of the day.
3. *Աւուր* or *յաւր* or *յօր*, to the day.
4. *զԱւր* or *զօր*, the day.
5. *յԱւրէ* or *յօրէ*, from the day.
6. *Աւուրբ*, with *or* by the day.

PLURAL

1. *Աւուրք*, the days.
2. *Աւուրց*, of the days.
3. *Աւուրց* or *յաւուրս*, to the days.
4. *զԱւուրս*, the days.
5. *յԱւուրց*, from the days.
6. *Աւուրբք*, with *or* by the days.

SINGULAR

1. *Հայր*, the father.
2. *Հաւր* or *Հօր*, of the father.

26

3. Հաւր, Հօր or գՀայր, to the father.
4. զՀայր, the father.
5. 'ի Հաւրէ or 'ի Հօրէ, from the father.
6. Հարբ, with *or* by the father.

1. Հարբ, the fathers.
2. Հարց or Հարանց, of the fathers.
3. Հարց, Հարանց or գՀարս, to the fathers.
4. զՀարս, the fathers.
5. 'ի Հարց or 'ի Հարանց, from the fathers.
6. Հարբբ, with *or* by the fathers.

1. Տիգրան, Tigranes.
2. Տիգրանայ, of Tigranes.
3. Տիգրանայ or 'ի Տիգրան, to Tigranes.
4. զՏիգրան, Tigranes.
5. 'ի Տիգրանայ, from Tigranes.
6. Տիգրանաւ, with *or* by Tigranes.

1. Հեղինէ, Helena.
2. Հեղինեայ, of Helena.
3. Հեղինեայ or առ Հեղինէ, to Helena.
4. զՀեղինէ, Helena.
5. 'ի Հեղինեայ, from Helena.
6. Հեղինեաւ, with *or* by Helena.

ADJECTIVE

An adjective is a word added to a Substantive to express its quality.

Adjectives in the Armenian language admit besides the number or case the degrees of comparison.

The Comparatives are formed in three modes; 1. with the particle *գոյն*, as *բարի*, good, *բարեգոյն*, better. *չար*, bad, *չարագոյն*, worse. *բազում*, much, many, *բազմագոյն*, more. 2. with the prepositions *քան*, *եւս*, *առ֊եւլ*, as, *մեծ*, great, *մեծ քան*, *մեծ եւս*, *առաւել'մեծ*, greater. 3. with different cases of the substantive, as, *մեծն մարգարէից*, greater than all prophets. *մեծն 'ի մարգարէս*, greater amongst the prophets.

The Superlatives are also formed in three manners: 1. with the particles *ամն* or *ամն*, *գեր*, *մեծ*, *երեք* or *ե*, put before them, as, *ամենաբարի*, best. *ամենիմաստուն*, wisest, *գերամաքուր*, most clean. *մեծավայելուչ*, most convenient. *երամեծ*, greatest. 2. by adding to them some adverbs, as, *եւս մեծագոյն* or *մեծագոյն եւս*, greatest. *յոյժ վատթարագոյն*, *անշնարին չար*, worst. *ամենելին գեղեցիկ*, most handsome. *երիցս եղ֊կելի*, most miserable. 3. by redoubling the positives, as, *մեծամեծ*, greatest. *չարաչար* or *չար առաւել քան դչար*, worst.

MIDDLE NOUNS

Those nouns are named *middle* or *mixed,*
which are neither Substantives nor Pronouns, and are classed generally in English
among the Adjectives.

They are of five kinds: Numeral, Parti-
tive, General, Interrogative, and Relative.

THE NOUNS NUMERAL

The nouns numeral are of five kinds: Ab-
solute, Cardinal, Separative, Distributive,
and Replicative.

ABSOLUTE

Մի or մին, մու, եզ, one.

Երկու, two.

Երեք, or եռ, երր, three.

Չորք or չորս, four.

Հինգ, five.

Վեց, six.

Եւթն or եօթն, seven.

Ութ, eight.

Ինն, nine.

Տասն, ten.

Մետասան, eleven.

Երկոտասան, twelve.

Երեքտասան, thirteen.

Չորեքտասան, fourteen.

Հնգետասան, fifteen.

Վեշտասան, sixteen.

Եւթներասն or եւթնուտասն, seventeen.

Ութեասն or ութուտասն, eighteen.

Իննեասն or իննուտասն, nineteen.

Քսան, twenty.

Քսան և մի, twenty one.

Երեսուն, thirty.

Երեսուն և երկու, thirty two.

Քառասուն, forty. *Karasoun*

Քառասուն և երեք, forty three.

Յիսուն, fifty. *Hès*

Յիսուն և չորք, fifty four.

Վաթսուն, sixty.

Եւթանասուն, seventy.

Ութսուն, eighty.

Իննսուն, ninety.

Իննսուն և ինն, ninety nine.

Հարիւր, hundred. *hoveur*

Երկերիւր, two hundred.

Երեքհարիւր, three hundred.

Չորեքհարիւր, four hundred.

Հինգհարիւր, five hundred.

Վեցհարիւր, six hundred.

Եւթնհարիւր, seven hundred.

Ութհարիւր, eight hundred.

Իննհարիւր, nine hundred.

Հազար, thousand. *ha zir*

Բիւր or բիւր, ten thousand.

CARDINAL

Առաջին or առաջնորդ, առաջներորդ, նախ-
  կին, նախինի, first.

Երկրորդ, second.

2^{v}

Երրորդ or երիր, *third.*
Չորրորդ or չորիր, քառորդ, *fourth.*
Հինգերորդ, *fifth.*
Վեցերորդ, *sixth.*
Եւթներորդ, *seventh.*
Ութերորդ, *eighth.*
Իններորդ, *ninth.*
Տասներորդ, *tenth.*
Քսաներորդ, *twentieth.*
Երեսներորդ, *thirtieth.*
Քառասներորդ, *fortieth.*
Յիսներորդ, *fiftieth.*
Վաթսներորդ, *sixtieth.*
Եւթանասներորդ, *seventieth.*
Ութսներորդ, *eightieth.*
Իննսներորդ, *ninetieth.*
Հարիւրերորդ, or Հարիւրորդ, *hundredth.*
Երկերիւրերորդ, *two hundredth.*
Հազարերորդ, *thousandth.*

SEPARATIVE

Միակ, *one, sole, only.*
Երկեակ or երկակ, *two only, two.*
Երրեակ, *three only, three.*
Չորեակ or քառեակ, *four only, four.*
Հնգեակ, *five only, five.*
Տասնեակ, *ten only, ten.*
Եւթանասնեակ, *seventy only, seventy.*
Հարիւրեակ, *hundred only, hundred.*

DISTRIBUTIVE

Երկոքեան or երկոքին, both, the two.
Երեքեան or երեքին, the three.
Չորեքեան or չորեքին, the four.
Եւթանեքեան or եւթանեքին, the seven.
Երկոտասանեքեան or երկոտասանեքին, the
    twelve.
Երկաքանչիւր, both, one and the other.

REPLICATIVE

Երկպատիկ or կրկին, double, two.
Երեքպատիկ, եռապատիկ or երեքկին, triple,
    treble, threefold.
Չորեքպատիկ, քառապատիկ or չորեքկին,
    fourfold.
Հնգապատիկ, quintuple, fivefold.
Եւթնապատիկ, sevenfold.
Տասնապատիկ, tenfold.
Հարիւրապատիկ, hundredfold.
Հազարապատիկ, thousandfold.

THE NOUNS PARTITIVE

Ոմն, ոք, իք, some, somebody, one, any,
    whosoever.
Ինչ, ինչ, a, one, some, certain, single, any.
Միմեանց or իրերաց, of one, of the other.
Իւրաքանչիւր or անցնիւր, each, every, any.
Մեւս or միւս, other, another.
Այլ ոք, այլ ոմն, another.
Այլ ինչ, այլ ինչ, another, different.

Մ*իւս ո*ն*, another.
Ի*րաքանչիւր ո*ք, every one.
Ի*րաքանչիւր ի*նչ, every or any thing.
Մ*ի մ*ի, every, any.
Քանի ի*նչ or քանի մ*ի, some, not many.

THE NOUNS GENERAL

Ա*մէնայն or ա*մէն, all, every, any.
Ա*մէնեքեան or ա*մէնեքին, all, every one.
Բ*ոլոր, all, whole, entire, total.
Բ*ոլորեքեան or բ*ոլորեքին, all, every one.
Հ*ամայն, հ*ամակ, հ*ամօրէն, բ*նաւ, ո*ղջոյն,
    all, whole, entire, total, complete.
Ա*մէնայն ո*ք, every one.
Ա*մէնայն ի*նչ, every or any thing.
Ո*ր ո*ք, whoever, whosoever.
Ո*ր ի*նչ, whatsoever.
Ո*չ ո*ք, none, not one, not any, nobody.
Ո*չ ի*նչ or ո*չ մ*ի ի*նչ, nothing, not any thing.

THE NOUNS INTERROGATIVE

Ո*° or ո*վ, who? which person?
Ո*ր, who? which?
Ի*նչ, what? which?
Քանի, how much? how many?
Ո*վ ո*ք, ո* ո*ք, ո*ր ո*ք, whoever? who?
Ո*ր ի*ն, զ*ի*նչ ի*նչ, whatever? what?
Ո*րպիսի, զ*ի*նպիսի, what? which?
Ո*րքան, ո*րչափ, how much? how many?

THE NOUNS RELATIVE

Այսպիսի, սոյնպիսի, *such, like, same, si-milar, as, so.*

Այդպիսի, դոյնպիսի, *so, as, like, similar.*

Այնպիսի, նոյնպիսի, *so, as, as that, like that.*

Այսքան, սոյնքան, *so much, as many.*

Այսչափ, սոյնչափ, *so much, as many.*

Այդքան, դոյնքան, *so many, so much.*

Այդչափ, դոյնչափ, *so many, so much.*

Այնքան, նոյնքան, *so many, so much.*

Այնչափ, նոյնչափ, *so many, so much, so much as.*

All these middle nouns are declined under one of the ten declensions of nouns substantive, except ոմն and ոք, which are differently declined in the singular, but similarly in the plural number, as

SINGULAR

1. Ոմն, one, some.   Ոք, one, any person.
2. Ուրումն, of one.   Ուրուք, of any.
3. Ումեմն, to one.   Ումեք, to any.
4. զՈմն, one.   զՈք, any.
5. յՈւմեմնէ, from one.   յՈւմեքէ, from any.
6. Ոմամբ, with or by one.   Ոմամբ, with or by any.

PLURAL

1. Ոմանք, some.
2. Ոմանց, of some.
3. Ոմանց or յոմանս, յոմանս, to some.
4. զՈմանս, some.
5. յՈմանց, from some.
6. Ոմամբք, with or by some.

PRONOUN

Pronouns stand in place of nouns and,
like them, have case, number, and particularly the first, second and third persons, as,
Ես, I. դու, thou. նա, he.

In Armenian they have no genders.

There are four kinds of pronouns: Substantive or Personal, as, Ես, I. դու, thou.
ինքն, he, himself. իր, own, himself. Definitive, as, սա, this (person or thing). դա, that
(person or thing). նա, that, he, she, it. Possessive, as, իմ or իմոյն, my, mine. մեր or
մերոյն, our, our's. քո or քոյն, thy, thine.
ձեր or ձերոյն, your, your's. իւր or իւրայ-
ին, his, hers, its. իւրեանց, their, their's.
And Relative, as, որ, who, which, that, what.

The three letters ս, դ, ն, are called Arti-
cles-distinctive-of-the-persons; and joined
to the terminations of words and verbs, shew
their persons or order, and are used as pronouns personal, possessive, and definitive, as,
մարդս, I who am a man, or my man, or this

man. *Մարդդ*, thou who art a man, or thy man, or that man. *Մարդն*, he who is a man, or his man or that man.

DECLENSIONS OF THE PERSONAL PRONOUNS

1. Person.

SINGULAR

1. Ես, I.
2. Իմ, of me, mine or my.
3. Ինձ, զիս, առ իս, to me.
4. զիս, me.
5. յինէն, from me.
6. ինեւ, with or by me.

PLURAL

1. Մեք, we.
2. Մեր, of us, our or our's.
3. Մեզ, զմեզ, առ մեզ, to us.
4. զմեզ, us.
5. ՚ի Մէնջ, from us.
6. Մեւք, or մեօք, with or by us.

2. Person.

SINGULAR

1. Դու, thou.
2. Քո, of thee, thine or thy.
3. Քեզ, առ քեզ, զքեզ, to thee.
4. զքեզ, thee.
5. ՚ի Քէն, from thee.
6. Քեւ, with or by thee.

1. Դուք *ye or* you.
2. Ձեր, of you, your *or* your's.
3. Ձեզ, ցձեզ, առ ձեզ, to you.
4. դձեզ, you.
5. ՚ի Ձէնք, from you.
6. Ձեւք or ձեօք, with *or* by you.

3. *Person.*

SINGULAR

1. ինքն, he *or* himself.   *entu*
2. ինքեան, of him *or* his.
3. ինքեան, or առ ինքն, to him.
4. դինքն, him.
5. յինքենէ, from him.
6. ինքեամբ, with *or* by him.

PLURAL

1. ինքեանք, they *or* themselves.
2. ինքեանց, of them, their *or* their's.
3. ինքեանց, or առ ինքեանս, to them.
4. դինքեանս, them.
5. յինքեանց, from them.
6. ինքեամբք, with *or* by them.

ինքն alone signifies *he, she,* but accompanied by another pronoun signifies *self,* as, ես ինքն, *myself.* դու ինքն, *thyself.* նա ինքն, *himself.*

1.
2. իր or իրեան, his.
3. իր, իրեան or առ իր, to him, to
    himself.
4.
5. յիրմէ, from him, from himself.
6. իրէ, իրեաւ or իրեամբ, with *or* by
    him *or* himself.

PLURAL

1.
2. իրեանց, their, their's.
3. իրեանց, to them *or* to themselves.
4.
5. յիրեանց, from them, from themselves.
6. իրեամբք, with *or* by them *or* themselves.

Declension of Definitive Pronouns Personal.

1. Person.

SINGULAR

1. Սա, this (person).
2. Սորա, of this.
3. Սմա or առ սա, to this.
4. զՍա, this.
5. 'ի Սմանէ, from this.
6. Սովաւ, with *or* by this.

1. Սոքա, these (persons).
2. Սոցա, of these.
3. Սոցա or առ սոսա, to these.
4. զՍոսա, these.
5. 'ի Սոցանէ, from these.
6. Սոքաւք or սոքօք, by *or* with these.

2. *Person.*

SINGULAR

1. Դա, that (person).
2. Դորա, of that.
3. Դմա or զդա, to that.
4. զԴա, that.
5. 'ի Դմանէ, from that.
6. Դովաւ, by *or* with that.

PLURAL

1. Դոքա, those (persons).
2. Դոցա, of those.
3. Դոցա or առ դոսա, to those.
4. զԴոսա, those.
5. 'ի Դոցանէ, from those.
6. Դոքաւք, or դոքօք, by *or* with those.

3. *Person.*

SINGULAR

1. Նա, that (person) he, she.
2. Նորա, of that.

3. Նմա, or ջնա, առ նա, to that.
4. զնա, that.
5. 'ի Նմանէ, from that.
6. Նովաւ, by or with that.

PLURAL

1. Նոքա, those.
2. Նոցա, of those.
3. Նոցա or առ նոսա, ջնոսա, to those.
4. զնոսա, those.
5. 'ի Նոցանէ, from those.
6. Նոքաւք or նոքօք, by or with those.

Declensions of Definitive Pronouns Adjective.

1. Person.

SINGULAR

1. Այս, this (person or thing).
2. Այսր or այսորիկ, of this.
3. Այսմ; այսմիկ or առ այս, to this.
4. զԱյս, this.
5. յԱյսմանէ, from this.
6. Այսու or այսուիկ, by or with this.

PLURAL

1. Այսք or այսոքիկ, these.
2. Այսց or այսոցիկ, of these.
3. Այսց, այսոցիկ or առ այսոսիկ, to these.
4. զԱյսոսիկ, these.
5. յԱյսց or յայսցանէ, from these.
6. Այսոքիւք or այսոքիմբք, by or with these.

2. *Person.*

1. Այդ, that (person *or* thing).
2. Այդր or այդորիկ, of that.
3. Այդմ, այդմիկ or առ այդ, to that.
4. զԱյդ, that.
5. յԱյդմանէ, from that.
6. Այդու or այդուիկ, by *or* with that.

1. Այդք or այդոքիկ, those.
2. Այդց or այդոցիկ, of those.
3. Այդց, այդոցիկ or առ այդոսիկ, to those.
4. զԱյդոսիկ, those.
5. յԱյդց or յայդցանէ, from those.
6. Այդոքիւք or այդոքիմբք, by *or* with those.

3. *Person.*

1. Այն, that (person *or* thing).
2. Այնր or այնորիկ, of that.
3. Այնմ, այնմիկ or առ այն, to that.
4. զԱյն, that.
5. յԱյնմանէ, from that.
6. Այնու or այնուիկ, by *or* with that.

1. Այնք or այնոքիկ, those.
2. Այնց or այնոցիկ, of those.

3. Այնց, այնոցիկ or առ այնոսիկ, յայնս, to those.
4. զԱյնոսիկ or զայնս, those.
5. յԱյնց or յայնցանէ, from those.
6. Այնոքիւք or այնոքիմբք, by or with those.

Other Definitive Pronouns Adjective.

1. Person.

SINGULAR

1. Սոյն, this same (person *or* thing).
2. Սորին or սորուն, of this same.
3. Սմին or առ սոյն, to this same.
4. զՍոյն, this same.
5. ('ի Սոյն or 'ի սմին) from this same.
6. Սովին or սովիմբ, by *or* with this same.

PLURAL

1. Սոյնք or սորին, these same.
2. Սոցին, սոցուն or սոցունց, of these same.
3. Սոցին or առ սոսին, առ սոյնս, to these same.
4. զՍոյնս, զսոսին, these same.
5. 'ի Սոցունց, from these same.
6. Սովիմբք, սոքիմբք, or սոքումբք, by or with these same.

2. *Person.*

1. Դոյն, that same (person *or* thing).
2. Դորին or դորունն, of that same.
3. Դմին or առ դոյն, to that same.
4. զԴոյն, that same.
5. (ի Դոյն or 'ի դմին) from that same.
6. Դովին or դովիմբ, by *or* with that same.

1. Դոյնք, or դոքին, those same.
2. Դոցին, դոցունն or դոցունց, of those same.
3. Դոցին or առ դոսին, առ դոյսա, to those same.
4. զԴոյսա or զդոսին, those same.
5. 'ի Դոցունց, from those same.
6. Դովիմբք, դոքիմբք or դոքումբք, by *or* with those same.

3. *Person.*

1. Նոյն, that same (person *or* thing).
2. Նորին or նորունն, of that same.
3. Նմին or առ նոյն, to that same.
4. զՆոյն, that same.
5. ('ի Նոյն or 'ի նմին) from that same.
6. Նովին or նովիմբ, by *or* with that same.

PLURAL

1. Նոյնք or ՆորիՆ, those same.
2. ՆոցիՆ, Նոցունն or Նոցունց, of those same.
3. Նոցին or առ Նոսին, առ Նոյնս, to those same.
4. զՆոյնս, or զՆոսին, those same.
5. ի Նոցունց, from those same.
6. Նովիմբք, Նորիմբք or Նոքումբք, by or with those same.

The Definitive pronouns are accompanied sometimes with the pronoun ինքն, *self*, as, սա ինքն, *this self-same.* դա ինքն, *that self-same or himself.* Նա ինքն, *that self-same or himself.* այս ինքն, *this same.* Նոյն ինքն, *same, that same.*

Or they are joined together, as, սոյն սա, *this same.* դոյն դա, դոյն այդ, *that same, the same himself.*

Declensions of Pronouns Possessive.

The Possessive pronouns are formed of personal and definitive pronouns; the second case of these forms the first case of the possessive.

1. *Person.*

SINGULAR

1. իմ, my (mine).
2. իմոյ, of my.

3. իմում, or առ իմ, to my.
4. զիմ, my.
5. յիմմէ or յիմոյ, from my.
6. իմով, by or with my.

PLURAL

1. իմք, my.
2. իմոց, of my.
3. իմոց, առ իմս, to my.
4. զիմս, my.
5. յիմոց, from my.
6. իմովք, by or with my.

SINGULAR

1. Մեր, our.
2. Մերոյ, of our, our's.
3. Մերում, to our.
4. զՄեր, our.
5. 'ի Մերմէ or 'ի մերոյ, from our.
6. Մերով, by or with our.

PLURAL

1. Մերք, our.
2. Մերոց, of our.
3. Մերոց, to our.
4. զՄերս, our.
5. 'ի Մերոց, from our.
6. Մերովք, by or with our.

2. Person.

SINGULAR

1. ‧քո, thy (thine).
2. ‧քոյ, of thy.
3. ‧քոյ, or քում, to thy.
4. զքո, thy.
5. 'ի քումմէ or 'ի քոյ, from thy.
6. ‧քով, by or with thy.

PLURAL

1. ‧քոյք, thy.
2. ‧քոց, of thy.
3. ‧քոց or 'ի քոյս, to thy.
4. զքոյս, thy.
5. 'ի քոց, from thy.
6. ‧քովք, by or with thy.

SINGULAR

1. Ձեր, your.
2. Ձերոյ, of your, your's.
3. Ձերում, to your.
4. զՁեր, your.
5. 'ի Ձերմէ or 'ի Ձերոյ, from your.
6. Ձերով, by or with your.

PLURAL

1. Ձերք, your.
2. Ձերոց, of your.
3. Ձերոց, to your.
4. զՁերս, your.

2*

5. 'ի Ձերոց, from your.
6. Ձերովք, by *or* with your.

3. *Person.*

1. իւր, his *or* her.
2. իւրոյ, of his.
3. իւրում, to his.
4. զիւր, his.
5. յիւրմէ or յիւրոյ, from his.
6. իւրով, by *or* with his.

1. իւրք, his.
2. իւրոց, of his.
3. իւրոց, to his.
4. զիւրս, his.
5. յիւրոց, from his.
6. իւրովք, by *or* with his.

From the genitives of these are formed
other possessives with a particle ն; they have
the same signification, but are declined with
prepositions, and are these: իմոյն, my,
mine. քոյն, thy, thine. մերոյն, our. ձերոյ-
ն, your. իւրոյն, his or her own.
The same possessives are formed also in
this manner: իմայն, my, mine. մերայն,
our. ձերայն, your. իւրայն, his. իւրեանն-
գային, their: and these are declined.

Declensions of possessives derived from the Definitives.

1. Person.

SINGULAR

1. Որա, his *or* her.
2. Որայոյ, of his.
3. Որայումֈ to his.
4.
5.
6. Որայով, by *or* with his.

PLURAL

1. Որայք, his *or* her.
2. Որայց *or* որայոց, of his.
3. Որայց, *or* որայոց, to his.
4. զՈրայս, his.
5. 'ի Որայոց, from his.
6. Որայովք, by *or* with his.

SINGULAR

1. Ոցա, their.
2. Ոցայոյ, of their.
3. Ոցայումֈ to their.
4.
5.
6. Ոցայով, by *or* with their.

PLURAL

1. Ոցայք, their.
2. Ոցայց *or* ոցայոց, of their.

3. Ունցայց or անցայող, to their.
4. զՈնցայս, their.
5. 'ի Ունցայող, from their.
6. Ունցայովբ, by or with their.

2. *Person.*

SINGULAR

1. Դորալ, his *or* her.
2. Դորայող, of his.
3. Դորայումֱ to his.
4.
5.
6. Դորայովֱ by *or* with his.

PLURAL

1. Դորայբ, his *or* her.
2. Դորայց or դորայող, of his.
3. Դորայց, դորայող or 'ի դորայս, to his.
4. զԴորայս, his.
5. 'ի Դորայող, from his.
6. Դորայովբ, by *or* with his.

SINGULAR

1. Դոցա, their.
2. Դոցայող, of their.
3. Դոցայումֱ to their.
4.
5.
6. Դոցայով, by *or* with their.

n arka(h)
G amayi
D — karkah ksarkah)
ac 3farka(h)

ah karkae
hstr. amayiu

n gam
ghram
g gyari   i gam ar gam
D —
ac 3 m gam
al i game
hstr gamau

Indic.   I am ... ... + ...   Perf.
   Pres.   Imp.
 sharj yem   sh ay ei   sharj yetze
       yeo   eir   yezy
       e   or   yeal
       yemk   eak   yelz
       ek   eik   yot
       yen   em   yer

 Subj.   ) ...
 Imp.   sharj yel
 Part Pres. sharj woth   a sharj yetz wogh
                                  yelz yeal
        Past { sharj yeal
                 yel wotz

1. Դոցայք, their.
2. Դոցայց or դոցայոց, of their.
3. Դոցայոց or ի դոցայս, to their.
4. զԴոցայս, their.
5. ի Դոցայոց, from their.
6. Դոցայովք, by or with their.

3. *Person.*

1. Նորա, his *or* her.
2. Նորայ, of his.
3. Նորայում, to his.
4.
5.
6. Նորայով, by *or* with his.

1. Նորայք, his *or* her.
2. Նորայց or նորայոց, of his.
3. Նորայց, նորայոց or ի նորայս, to his.
4. զՆորայս, his.
5. ի Նորայոց, from his.
6. Նորայովք, by *or* with his.

1. Նոցա, their.
2. Նոցայոց, of their.
3. Նոցայում, to their.
4.
5.
6. Նոցայով, by *or* with their.

50

1. Նոցայք, their.
2. Նոցայց or Նոցայոց, of their.
3. Նոցայոց or 'ի Նոցայս, to their.
4. զՆոցայս, their.
5. 'ի Նոցայոց, from their.
6. Նոցայովք, by or with their.

Declension of the Pronoun Relative.

SINGULAR

1. Որ or ո, who, which, what, that.
2. Որոյ, whose, of which.
3. Որում or առ որ, to whom, to which.
4. զՈր, whom.
5. յՈրմէ or յորոյ, from whom, from which.
6. Որով, with or by whom or which.

PLURAL

1. Որք, who, which, what, that.
2. Որոց, whose, of which.
3. Որոց or առ որս, to which.
4. զՈրս, which.
5. յՈրոց, from which.
6. Որովք, by or with which.

VERB

The verb signifies to be, to do, or to suffer with tense, number and person.

Five properties belong to the verb. Kind,

Tense *or* Time, Number, Person and Conjugation.

There are four kinds of verbs: Substantive, Active, Passive, and Neutral.

The first denotes existence, as, *եմ, I am. գոմ, I do exist.* The second action, as, *առնեմ, I do, I make.* The third sufferance, as, *առնիմ, I am done* or *made.* The fourth the action subsisting in itself, as, *աշխատիմ, I labour. գնամ, I go.*

There is also another kind called Common, which signifies the action as well as the sufferance, as, *դատիմ, I judge,* and *I am judged.*

There are three tenses of the verb: the Present, as, *գրեմ, I write.* Past, as, *գրեցի, I wrote:* and Future, as, *գրեցից, I shall write.*

The past is either Imperfect, as, *գրէի, I was writing,* or Perfect, as, *գրեցի, I wrote.*

The ancient grammarians add two other perfect tenses: the Preter-perfect, as, *գրեալ եմ, I have written,* and the Preter-plu-perfect, as, *գրեալ էի, I had written:* but these tenses do not necessarily belong to the Armenian language.

NUMBER

The verb has two numbers: Singular, as, *գրեմ*, I *write*, and Plural, as, *գրեմք*, *we write.*

PERSON

The persons are three: First, as, *գրեմ*, I *write.* Second, as, *գրես*, *thou writest.* and Third, as, *գրէ*, *he writes.*

CONJUGATION

The variation of a verb in it's tenses, numbers, and persons is called conjugation.

Conjugation is either Regular or Irregular.

Regular conjugation changes regularly in the termination of the verb without any omission.

The irregular conjugation wants some tense or mood, and is called *Defective;* or in some tense or mood deviates from the rule, and is called *Devious;* or wants the first and second person, and is called *Impersonal.*

MOODS OF THE VERB

The manner of signifying some action is called the Mood. There are four in the regular verbs: Indicative, Imperative, Subjunctive and Infinitive.

When the verb indicates some action, affirming it simply, it is called the indicative, as, *գրեմ*, I write. *գրեցի*, I wrote. *գրեցից*, I shall write.

When it commands or prohibits, it is called imperative, as, *գրեա*, write thou or do thou write. *Մի գրեր*, do thou write not.

When it expresses a suspended action, or dependent upon another verb to complete the sense, it is called subjunctive, as, *եթէ գրիցեմ*, if I write.

When one action is denoted without tense, number or person, the mood is called infinitive, as, *գրել*, to write.

The indicative has three tenses, with persons and numbers. The imperative has two tenses: present, and future; it has two numbers, but in the singular has no first person, because he who speaks does not command himself. However in the plural there is a first person, because other persons are addressed and commanded.

The subjunctive has the numbers, and persons perfect: but in the tenses has only the present, and the future, because the Armenian language has not properly the past tense of subjunctive.

The infinitive has neither tense, number, nor person: whence it is used as a noun, and declined in the singular, and is then called the Gerund.

Example.

1. Գրել, to write.
2. Գրելոյ, of writing.
3. Գրելոյ or ՚ի գրել, to writing.
4. զԳրել, the writing.
5. ՚ի Գրելոյ, from writing.
6. Գրելով, with *or* by writing, writing.

The Conjugations of the verbs are four, and are distinguished by the last vowels of their indicatives, which are, ե, ա, ու, ի.

The indicative of the first conjugation ends with the vowel ե, as, շարժեմ, *I move;* of the second with ա, as, լուանամ, *I wash;* of the third with ու, as, հեղում, *I pour out;* of the fourth with ի, as, ուսանիմ, *I learn.*

Every conjugation although different in its moods, tenses, numbers and persons, preserves the first syllable of it's indicative, excepting such verbs as are Devious.

Every person and tense of the verb ending in ք or ն, is plural. ք is the sign of the first and second person, and ն of the third; provided only that ն be not the article distinctive of the person, because it then would be singular.

Every verb which terminates in մ, is in the first person; in ս, is in the second person; verbs ending in է or ց, are in the first

or second person; verbs ending in Ե, ա,
ո, ա, or ան, in the third person; and those
terminating in ր, are in the second and third
person.

In every conjugation the future of the indicative is formed by adding the letter ց to
the perfect, as, շարժեցի, I moved, շարժե
ցից, I shall move. լուացի, I washed, լուա
ցից, I shall wash. Հեղի, I poured out, Հե
ղից, I shall pour out. ուսայ, I learned, ու
սայց, I shall learn.

PARTICIPLE

The participle is formed by adding to
the termination of the verb the particles ող
or ող (sign of the present), եալ (sign of the
past) ից or լի (sign of the future).

As a verb it has tense, and as a noun,
cases and numbers.

Example.

PRESENT

Singular.

1. Գրող or գրող, he who writes, or is
   writing.
2. Գրողի, of him who writes.
3. Գրողի or առ գրողն, to him who writes.
4. զԳրող, him who writes.

53

5. 'ի Գրողէ, from him who writes.
6. Գրողաւ, by or with him who writes.

Plural.

1. Գրողք, those who write, or who are writing.
2. Գրողաց, of those who write.
3. Գրողաց or առ գրողս, to those who write.
4. զԳրողս, those who write.
5. 'ի Գրողաց, from those who write.
6. Գրողաւք or գրողօք, by or with those who write.

Singular.

1. Գրեալ, written or wrote.
2. Գրելոյ, of written.
3. Գրելոյ or առ գրեալն, to written.
4. զԳրեալն, written.
5. 'ի Գրելոյ, from written.
6. Գրելով, by or with written.

Plural.

1. Գրեալք, written or wrote.
2. Գրելոց, of written.
3. Գրելոց or առ գրեալս, to written.
4. զԳրեալս, written.
5. 'ի Գրելոց, from written.
6. Գրելովք, by or with written.

The future ending in գ, is declined only
with prepositions, as,

Singular.

1. գրելոյ, to be written.
3. 'ի գրելոյ, to that to be written.
4. զգրելոյ, to be written.

Plural.

1. գրելոյք, to be written.
3. 'ի գրելոյս, to that to be written.
4. զգրելոյս, to be written.

The future terminated in լի, is declined
thus,

Singular.

1. գրելի, to be written.
2. գրելւոյ, of that to be written.
3. գրելւոյ or առ գրելի, to that to be
    written.
4. զգրելի, to be written.
5. 'ի գրելւոյ, from that to be written.
6. գրելեաւ, by *or* with that to be written.

Plural.

1. գրելիք, to be written.
2. գրելեաց, of that to be written.
3. գրելեաց or 'ի գրելիս, to that to be
    written.
4. զգրելիս, to be written.

5. 'ի Գրելեաց, from that to be written.

6. Գրելեաւբ or գրելեօբ, by or with that to be written.

Specimen of the four conjugations of the verbs regular with their moods, tenses, numbers and persons.

INDICATIVE

Present.

Sing. Pers.	Plur. Pers.
1. Շարժ–եմ–ես–է.	եմբ–էբ–են.
2. Լուան–ամ–աս–այ.	ամբ–այբ–ան.
3. Հեղ–ում–ուս–ու.	ումբ–ույբ–ուն.
4. Ոսան–իմ–իս–ի.	իմբ–իբ–ին.

Imperfect.

1. Շարժ–էի–էիր–էր.	էաբ–էիբ–էին.
2. Լուան–այի–այիր–այր.	այաբ–այիբ–ային.
3. Հեղ–ուի–ուիր–այր.	ուաբ–ուիբ–ուին.
4. Ոսան–էի–էիր–էր.	էաբ–էիբ–էին.

Perfect.

1. Շարժ–եցի–եցեր–եաց.	եցաբ–եցիբ–եցին.
2. Լուա–ցի–ցեր–լուաց.	ցաբ–ցիբ–ցին.
3. Հեղ–ի–եր–հեղ.	աբ–իբ–ին.
4. Ոս–այր–ար–աւ.	աբ–այբ–ան.

Future.

1. Շարժ–եցից–եսցես–եսցէ.	եսցուբ–եսջիբ–եսցեն.
2. Լուա–ցից–ացես–ացէ.	ացուբ–ասջիբ–ացեն.
3. Հեղ–ից–ցես–ցէ.	ցուբ–ջիբ–ցեն.
4. Ոս–այց–ցես–ցի.	յուբ–ջիբ–ցին.

IMPERATIVE

Present.

1. Բարձեա՛, մի՛ շարժեր.   Բարձեցէ՛ք, մի՛ շարժէք.
   Բարձեսցէ՛, մի՛ շարժեսցէ.   Բարձեսցե՛ն, մի՛ շարժեսցեն.
2. Լուա՛, մի՛ լուանար.   Լուացէ՛ք, մի՛ լուանայք.
   Լուասցէ՛, մի՛ լուասցէ.   Լուասցե՛ն, մի՛ լուասցեն.
3. Հե՛ղ, մի՛ հեղուր.   Հեղէ՛ք, մի՛ հեղուք.
   Հեղցէ՛, մի՛ հեղցէ.   Հեղցե՛ն, մի՛ հեղցեն.
4. Ուսի՛ր, մի՛ ուսանիր.   Ուսարո՛ւք, մի՛ ուսանիք.
   Ուսցի՛, մի՛ ուսցի.   Ուսցի՛ն, մի՛ ուսցին.

Future.

1. Բարձեսցի՛ր or շարժես.   Բարձեսցո՛ւք, շարժեսցի՛ք,
   ցես, շարժեսցէ.   շարժեսցեն.
2. Լուասցի՛ր or լուասցես, Լուասցո՛ւք,   լուասցի՛ք,
   լուասցէ.   լուասցեն.
3. Հեղցի՛ր or հեղցես, հեղ Հեղցո՛ւք, հեղցի՛ք, հեղ
   ցէ.   ցեն.
4. Ուսցի՛ր or ուսանիցի՛ր, Ուսցո՛ւք, ուսցի՛ք or ուսա
   ուսցի.   նիցի՛ք, ուսցին.

SUBJUNCTIVE

The present is formed like that of indicative.

Future.

1. Բարձ-իցեմ-իցես-իցէ.   իցեմք-իցէք-իցեն.
2. Լուան-այցեմ-այցես-այցէ.   այցեմք-այցէք-այցեն.
3. Հեղ-ուցում-ուցուս-ուցու. ուցումք-ուցուք-ուցուն.
4. Ուսան-իցիմ-իցիս-իցի.   իցիմք-իցիք-իցին.

INFINITIVE

1. Բարձ-ել.
2. Լուան-ալ.
3. Հեղ-ուլ.
4. Ուսան-իլ or ել.

PARTICIPLE

Present.

 Շարժող or Շարժեցող․ Լուացող․ Հեղող․ Ուսանող․

Past.

Շարժեալ․ Լուացեալ․ Հեղեալ․ Ուսեալ․

Future.

Շարժելոց or Շարժելի․ Լուանալոց or Լուանալի․
Հեղլոց or Հեղլի․ Ուսանելոց or Ուսանելի։

CONJUGATION OF SUBSTANTIVE VERBS

Defective verb եմ, I am.

INDICATIVE

Present.

եմ, I am. ես, thou art. է, he is.
եմք, we are. էք, ye are. են, they are.

Imperfect.

Էի, I was. Էիր, thou wast. Էր, he was.
Էաք, we were. Էիք, ye were. Էին, they
were.

IMPERATIVE

Եր, be thou or do thou be.
Էք, or երուք, be ye or do ye be.

SUBJUNCTIVE

]*ԻյԷմ,* I be. *ԻյԷս,* thou be. * Իյէ,* he be.
]*Իյէմք,* we be. *Իյէք,* ye be. * Իյէն,* they be.

INFINITIVE

Ել, to be.

PARTICIPLE

Past.

Եալ, been *or* having been.

Future.

Ելոց, which is to be, *or* about to be.

Comparing this verb with the verb շարժել, *to move,* of the first conjugation, it is
clearly seen, that its conjugation is the basis
of the latter.

Defective verb Գոմ, *I am or I exist.*

INDICATIVE

Present.

Գոմ, I am. *գոս,* thou art. *գոյ,* he is.
Գոմք, we are. *գոյք,* ye are. *գոն,* they are.

Imperfect.

Գոյիր, thou wast. *գոյր,* he was.
Գոյին, they were.

62

SUBJUNCTIVE

Future.

Գուցէ, he be, it may be, it would be.
Գուցեն, they be, they may be.

INFINITIVE

Գոլ, to be, to exist.

PARTICIPLE

Present.

Գոյող, being.
The deficiencies of this verb are supplied
by the means of the other substantive verbs.
The word չիք is used sometimes as a substantive verb, as, չիք իմ այր, I have no husband, or I am without a husband, or I am
not married. ուսեալ բնաւ չիք, he has never learned.

Substantive verb Եղանիմ, I am made or
done.

INDICATIVE

Present.

Եղանիմ, I am made. Եղանիս, thou art
made. Եղանի, he is made.
Եղանիմք, we are made. Եղանիք, ye are
made. Եղանին, they are made.

Imperfect.

Եղանէի, I was made. Եղանէիր, thou wast made. Եղանէր, he was made.
Եղանէաք, we were made. Եղանէիք, ye were made. Եղանէին, they were made.

Perfect.

Եղէ or Եղայ, I have been. Եղէր, thou hast been. Եղև, he has been.
Եղաք, or Եղէաք, we have been. Եղէք, or Եղայք, ye have been. Եղէն, they have been.

Future.

Եղէց, I shall be. Եղիցիս, thou shalt be. Եղիցի, he shall be.

IMPERATIVE

Present.

Մի եղանիր, be thou not. Եղիցի, let him be. Եղերուք, be ye. Մի եղանիք, be ye not. Եղիցին, let them be.

SUBJUNCTIVE

The present is formed like that of the Indicative.

Future.

Եղիցիմ or Եղանիցիմ, I shall be made. Եղիցիս, thou shalt be made. Եղիցի, he shall be made.

Եղիցիմք or Եղանիցիմք, we shall be made. Եղիցիք, ye shall be made. Եղիցին, they shall be made.

INFINITIVE

Եղանիլ, to be, to be made, to be done.

PARTICIPLE

Past.

Եղեալ, been, made, done, having been.

Future.

Եղանելոց or Եղանելի, which is to be.

Substantive verb Լինեմ, *I am, I am made. or done.*

INDICATIVE

Present.

Լինիմ, I am. լինիս, thou art. լինի, he is.
Լինիմք, we are. լինիք, ye are. լինին, they are.

Imperfect.

Լինէի, I was. լինէիր, thou wast. լինէր, he was. ·
Լինէաք, we were. լինէիք, ye were. լինէին, they were.

Future.

Լիցիմ, I shall be. լիցիս, thou shalt be. լիցի, he shall be.

Լիցուք, we shall be. լիջիք or լիջիք, ye shall be. լիցին, they shall be.

Present.

Լեր, be thou. մի լինիր, be thou not. լիցի, let him be.

Լիք, or լերուք, be ye. մի լինիք, be ye not. լիցին, let them be.

Future.

Լիջիր or լինիջիր or լիցիս, be thou. լիցի, let him be.

Լիցուք, let us be. լիջիք, or լինիջիք, be ye. լիցին, let them be.

Present is like that of the Indicative.

Future.

Լինիցիմ, I be or may be. լինիցիս, thou be. լինիցի, he be.

Լինիցուք, we be. լինիցիք, ye be. լինիցին, they be.

Լինել, to be.

PARTICIPLE

Present.

Լինող, being.

Past.

Եալ or լինեալ, been, having been.

Future.

Լինելոց or լինելի, which is to be.

FIRST CONJUGATION

Active Շարժել, To move.

INDICATIVE

sharjyem

Present.

Շարժեմ, I move. Շարժես, thou movest.
Շարժէ, he moves.
Շարժեմք, we move. Շարժէք, ye move.
Շարժեն, they move.

Imperfect.

Շարժէի, I moved *or* was moving. Շար-
ժէիր, thou movedst *or* wast moving, Շար-
ժէր, he moved *or* was moving.
Շարժէաք, we moved *or* were moving.
Շարժէիք, ye moved *or* were moving. Շար-
ժէին, they moved *or* were moving.

Perfect.

 Շարժեցի, I moved. շարժեցեր, thou movedst. շարժեաց, he moved.
Շարժեցաք, we moved. շարժեցիք, ye moved. շարժեցին, they moved.

As we have remarked above, the Preter-
perfect, and Preter-plu-perfect are not properly formed in the Armenian language, because when the necessity occurs, they are
accustomed to join the participle to the other
tenses of the verb substantive.

Future.

Շարժեցից, I shall move. շարժեսցես, thou
shalt move. շարժեսցէ, he shall move.
Շարժեսցուք, we shall move. շարժեսցիք,
ye shall move. շարժեսցեն, they shall
move.

IMPERATIVE

Present.

Շարժեա, move thou. մի շարժեր, move
thou not. շարժեսցէ, let him move.
Շարժեցէք, move ye. մի շարժէք, move ye
not. շարժեսցեն, let them move.

The negative particle մի, not, is also
placed with the third person of the present,
and before all the persons of the future in
every conjugation.

Future.

Շարժեաջիր or շարժեացես, move thou. շարժեացէ, let him move.

Շարժեացուք, let us move. շարժեաջիք, move ye. շարժեացէն, let them move.

SUBJUNCTIVE

The present is like that of the Indicative.

Future.

Շարժիցեմ, I move, I may, might, could, should, would move. շարժիցես, thou move, etc. շարժիցէ, he move, etc.

Շարժիցեմք, we move, etc. շարժիցէք, ye move, etc. շարժիցեն, they move, etc.

The future of the indicative, of the imperative, and of the subjunctive from their affinity are adopted by turns in all the four conjugations.

INFINITIVE

Շարժել, to move.

PARTICIPLE

Present.

Շարժող or շարժեցող, moving, who moves.

Past.

Շարժեալ or շարժեցեալ, having moved.

Future.

Ζωրժելոց, which has to move.

All the verbs active and neuter-active, which in the first person of the perfect end in եցի or ացի, are thus conjugated; and also the verbs Transitive ending in ուցի.

Passive Ζωրժիլ, *To be moved.*

The Passive of the first conjugation is formed by changing the ե in the last syllable of the Active into ի; the ցի into ցայ; the եց into աց: besides a few other variations.

Present.

Ζωրժիմ, I am moved. ζωրժիս, thou art moved. ζωրժի, he is moved.
Ζωրժիմք, we are moved. ζωրժիք, ye are moved. ζωրժին, they are moved.

Imperfect.

Ζωրժէի, I was moved. ζωրժէիր, thou wast moved. ζωրժէր or ζωրժիւր, he was moved.
Ζωրժէաք, we were moved. ζωրժէիք, ye were moved. ζωրժէին, they were moved.

Perfect.

Շարժեցայ, I have been moved. շարժեցար, thou hast been moved. շարժեցաւ, he has been moved.

Շարժեցաք, we have been moved. շարժեցայք, ye have been moved. շարժեցան, they have been moved.

Future.

Շարժեցայց, I shall be moved. շարժեսցիս, thou shalt be moved. շարժեսցի, he shall be moved.

Շարժեսցուք, we shall be moved. շարժիցիք, ye shall bo moved. շարժեսցին, they shall be moved.

IMPERATIVE

Present.

Շարժեաց or շարժեցիր, be thou moved. մի՛ շարժիր, be thou not moved. շարժեսցի, let him be moved.

Շարժեցարուք, be ye moved. մի՛ շարժիք, be ye not moved. շարժեսցին, let them be moved.

Future.

Շարժեսցիր or շարժիցիր, be thou moved. շարժեսցի, let him be moved.

Շարժեսցուք, let us be moved. շարժիցիք, be ye moved. շարժեսցին, let them be moved.

Present is like that of the Indicative.

Future.

Շարժիցիմ, I shall be moved. շարժիցիս, thou shalt be moved. շարժիցի, he shall be moved.

Շարժիցիմք, we shall be moved. շարժիցիք, ye shall be moved. շարժիցին, they shall be moved.

INFINITIVE

Շարժիլ or շարժել, to be moved.

PARTICIPLE

Past.

Շարժեալ or շարժեցեալ, moved, being moved.

Future.

Շարժելոց or շարժելի, which is to be moved.

In this manner many Neuter-passive and Common verbs are conjugated.

SECOND CONJUGATION

Active Լուանալ, *To wash.*

INDICATIVE

Present.

Լուանամ, I wash. Լուանաս, thou washest.
Լուանայ, he washeth.
Լուանամք, we wash. Լուանայք, ye wash.
Լուանան, they wash.

Imperfect.

Լուանայի, I washed *or* was washing. Լուա-
նայիր, thou washedst *or* wast washing.
Լուանայր, he washed *or* was washing.
Լուանայաք, we washed *or* were washing.
Լուանայիք, ye washed *or* were washing.
Լուանային, they washed *or* were washing.

Perfect.

Լուացի, I washed. Լուացեր, thou washedst.
Լուաց, he washed.
Լուացաք, we washed. Լուացէք, ye washed.
Լուացին, they washed.

Future.

Լուացից, I shall wash. Լուացես, thou shalt
wash. Լուացէ, he shall wash.
Լուացուք, we shall wash. Լուացջիք, ye
shall wash. Լուացեն, they shall wash.

IMPERATIVE

Present and *Future.*

Լուա՛, լուաշ՛ի՛ր, or լուացե՛ս, wash thou. Մի՛ լուանար, wash thou not. լուացէ՛, let him wash.

Լուասցո՛ւք, let us wash. լուացէ՛ք, or լուաշ՛ի՛ք, wash ye. լուացէ՛ն, let them wash.

SUBJUNCTIVE

Future.

Լուանայցեմ, I wash, may wash, might wash, I could, should, would wash. լուանայցես, thou wash, *etc.* լուանայցէ, he wash, *etc.* Լուանայցեմք, we wash. լուանայցէք, ye wash. լուանայցեն, they wash.

INFINITIVE

Լուանալ, to wash.

PARTICIPLE

Present.

Լուացող, washing, who washes.

Past.

Լուացեալ, having washed.

Future.

Լուանալոց, who has to wash.

Thus also are conjugated the verbs, which in the first person of the Perfect terminate in ցայ.

74

Passive Լուանիլ, *To be washed.*

INDICATIVE

Present.

Լուանիմ, I am washed. լուանիս, thou art washed. լուանի, he is washed.
Լուանիմք, we are washed. լուանիք, ye are washed. լուանին, they are washed.

Perfect.

Լուացայ, I have been washed. լուացար, thou hast been washed. լուացաւ, he has been washed.
Լուացաք, we have been washed. լուացայք, ye have been washed. լուացան, they have been washed.

Future.

Լուացայց, I shall be washed. լուասցիս, thou shalt be washed. լուասցի, he shall be washed.
Լուասցուք, we shall be washed. լուասջիք, ye shall be washed. լուասցին, they shall be washed.

IMPERATIVE

Present and *Future.*

Լուա, լուացիր or լուասջիր, be thou washed. լուասցի, let him be washed.

Լուացուք, let us be washed. լուաջիք, be ye washed. լուացին, let them be washed.

Լուանայցիմ, I may be washed. լուանայցիս, thou may est be washed. լուանայցի, he may be washed.

Լուանայցիմք, we may be washed. լուանայցիք, ye may be washed. լուանայցին, they may be washed.

Լուանիլ, to be washed.

Past.

Լուացեալ, washed.

Future.

Լուանալի, which is to be washed.

The Passives of the second conjugation are not so harmonious to the ear, whence they are sometimes formed by means of the verbs substantive, or the actives are adopted with a passive sense.

THIRD CONJUGATION

Active Հեղուլ, *To pour out.*

INDICATIVE

Present.

Հեղում, I pour out. Հեղուս, thou pourest out. Հեղու, he pours out.

Հեղումք, we pour out. Հեղուք, ye pour out. Հեղուն, they pour out.

Imperfect.

Հեղուի, I poured out *or* was pouring out. Հեղուիր, thou pour'dst out *or* wast pouring out. Հեղոյր, he poured out *or* was pouring out.

Հեղուաք, we poured out *or* were pouring out. Հեղուիք, ye poured out *or* were pouring out. Հեղուին, they poured out *or* were pouring out.

Perfect.

Հեղի, I poured out. Հեղեր, thou pour'dst out. եհեղ or հեղ, he poured out.

Հեղաք, we poured out. Հեղիք, ye poured out. Հեղին, they poured out.

Future.

Հեղից, I shall pour out. Հեղցես, thou shalt pour out. Հեղցէ, he shall pour out.

Հեղցունք, we shall pour out. Հեղջիք, ye shall pour out. Հեղցեն, they shall pour out.

IMPERATIVE

Present and *Future*

Հեղ, Հեղջիր, or Հեղցես, do thou pour out. Մի Հեղուր, do thou not pour out. Հեղցէ, let him pour out.

Հեղցուք, let us pour out. Հեղէք, or Հեղջիք, do ye pour out. Մի Հեղուք, do ye not pour out. Հեղցեն, let them pour out.

SUBJUNCTIVE

Future.

Հեղուցում, I pour out, I may, might, could, should, would pour out. Հեղուցուս, thou pour out, *etc.* Հեղուցու, he pour out, *etc.* Հեղուցուք, we pour out, *etc.* Հեղուցուք, ye pour out. Հեղուցուն, they pour out.

INFINITIVE

Հեղուլ, to pour out.

PARTICIPLE

Present.

Հեղող, pouring out.

Past.

Հեղեալ, having poured out.

Future.

Հեղլոց, who has to pour out.

In this manner also are conjugated the verbs which in the first person of the Perfect terminate in այ or եայ.

Passive Հեղանիլ, *To be poured out.*

INDICATIVE

Present.

Հեղանիմ, I am poured out. Հեղանիս, thou art poured out. Հեղանի, he is poured out. Հեղանիմք, we are poured out. Հեղանիք, ye are poured out. Հեղանին, they are poured out.

Perfect.

Հեղայ, I have been poured out. Հեղար, thou hast been poured out. Հեղաւ, he has been poured out. Հեղաք, we have been poured out. Հեղայք, ye have been poured out. Հեղան, they have been poured out.

Future.

Հեղայց, I shall be poured out. Հեղցիս, thou shalt be poured out. Հեղցի, he shall be poured out. Հեղցուք, we shall be poured out. Հեղջիք, ye shall be poured out. Հեղցին, they shall be poured out.

IMPERATIVE

* Հեղիր* or *Հեղցիս*, be thou poured out.
Հեղցի, let him be poured out.
Հեղարուք or *Հեղջիք*, be ye poured out.
Հեղցին, let them be poured out.

INFINITIVE

Հեղանիլ, to be poured out.

PARTICIPLE

Past.

Հեղեալ, poured out.

Future.

Հեղլի, which is to be poured out.

The deficiencies of the third conjugation passive are supplied from it's active.

FOURTH CONJUGATION

Common verb *Ուսանիլ*, *To learn.*

INDICATIVE

Present.

Ուսանիմ, I learn. *ուսանիս*, thou learnest.
ուսանի, he learns.
Ուսանիմք, we learn. *ուսանիք*, ye learn.
ուսանին, they learn.

Imperfect.

Ուսանէի, I learned *or* was learning. Ուսա_
նէիր, thou learnedst *or* wast learning.
ուսանէր, he learned *or* was learning.
Ուսանէաք, we learned *or* were learning.
ուսանէիք, ye learned *or* were learning.
ուսանէին, they learned *or* were learning.

Perfect.

Ուսայ, I have learned. ուսար, thou hast
learned. ուսաւ, he has learned.
Ուսաք, we have learned. ուսայք, ye have
learned. ուսան, they have learned.

Future.

Ուսայց, I shall learn. ուսցիս, thou shalt
learn. ուսցի, he shall learn.
Ուսցուք, we shall learn. ուսցիք, ye shall
learn. ուսցին, they shall learn.

IMPERATIVE

Present.

Ուսիր, learn thou. մի ուսանիր, learn thou
not. ուսցի, let him learn.
Ուսարուք, do ye learn. մի ուսանիք, do ye
not learn. ուսցին, let them learn.

Future.

Ուսցիր, or ուսանիցիր, learn thou. ուսցի,
let him learn.

Ուցնւք, let us learn. ուջիք or ուսանիջիք, do ye learn. ուցին, let them learn.

SUBJUNCTIVE

The Present is like that of the Indicative.

Future.

Ուսանիցիմ, I learn, may, might, could, should, would learn. ուսանիցիս, thou learn, etc. ուսանիցի, he learn, etc. Ուսանիցիմք, we learn. ուսանիցիք, ye learn. ուսանիցին, they learn.

INFINITIVE

Ուսանիլ, or ուսանել, to learn.

PARTICIPLE

Present.

Ուսանող, learning, who learns.

Past.

Ուեալ, having learned.

Future.

Ուսանելոց or ուսանելի, who has to learn.

Thus are also conjugated the common verbs which in the first person of the Perfect terminate in այ.

They are at the same time active and passive.

5*

Conjugations of the Irregular verbs.

ACTIVE

INDICATIVE

Present.

Առնեմ, I make. առնես, thou makest. առնէ, he makes.
Առնեմք, we make. առնէք, ye make. առնեն, they make.

Perfect.

Արարի, I have made. արարեր, thou hast made. արար, he has made.

INFINITIVE

Առնել, to make, to do.

PARTICIPLE

Present.

Արարող or առնող, making, who makes.

Past.

Արարեալ, having made, making.

Future.

Առնելոց, who has to make.

PASSIVE

INDICATIVE

Present.

Առնիմ, I am made. առնիս, thou art made. առնի, he is made.

Առնիմք, we are made. առնիք, ye are made. առնին, they are made.

Perfect.

Արարայ, I have been made. արարար, thou hast been made. արարաւ, he has been made.

Արարաք, we have been made. արարայք, ye have been made. արարան, they have been made.

INFINITIVE

Առնիլ, to be made.

PARTICIPLE

Past.

Արարեալ, (not արարեցեալ) made.

Future.

Առնելի or առնելոց, which is to be made.

ACTIVE

INDICATIVE

Present.

դնեմ, I put. դնես, thou putst. դնէ, he puts. դնեմք, we put. դնէք, ye put. դնեն, they put.

Perfect.

եդի, I have put. եդիր or եդեր, thou hast put. եդ, he has put. եդաք, we have put. եդիք, ye have put. եդին, they have put.

INFINITIVE

դնել, to put, to place.

PARTICIPLE

Present.

դնող, putting.

Past.

եդեալ, having put.

Future.

դնելոց, who has to put.

PASSIVE

INDICATIVE

Present.

դնիմ, I am put. դնիս, thou art put. դնի, he is put.

Դնիմք, we are put. *դնիք*, ye are put. *դնին*,
they are put.

Perfect.

Եդայ, I have been put. *Եդար*, thou hast
been put. *Եդաւ*, he has been put.
Եդաք, we have been put. *Եդայք*, ye have
been put. *Եդան*, they have been put.

INFINITIVE

Դնիլ, to be put.

PARTICIPLE

Past.

Եդեալ (not *դրեցեալ*) put.

Future.

Դնելի or *դնելոց*, which is to be put.

ACTIVE

INDICATIVE

Present.

Լսեմ, I hear. *լսես*, thou hearest. *լսէ*, he
hears.
Լսեմք, we hear. *լսէք*, ye hear. *լսեն*, they
hear.

Perfect.

Լուայ, I heard. *լուար*, thou heard. *լուաւ*,
he heard.

Լուաք, we heard. Լուայք, ye heard. Լուան, they heard.

INFINITIVE

Լսել, to hear.

PARTICIPLE

Present.

Լսող, hearing, who hears.

Past.

Լուեալ, having heared, hearing.

Future.

Լսելոց, who has to hear.

PASSIVE

INDICATIVE

Present.

Լսիմ, I am heard. լսիս, thou art heard. լսի, he *or* it is heard.

Լսիմք, we are heard. լսիք, ye are heard. լսին, they are heard.

Perfect.

Is formed by means of the Substantive verb, as,

Լուեալ, լսելի, լուր or լու եղէ, I have been heard. լուեալ եղեր, thou hast been heard. լուեալ եղե, he has been heard.

Լուեալ, լսէիր, լուր or լու եղաք, we have been heard. լուեալ եղէք, ye have been heard. լուեալ եղեն, they have been heard.

INFINITIVE

լսիլ, to be heard.

PARTICIPLE

Past.

լուեալ, heard.

Future.

լսելի, which is to be heard.

This verb is also regular.

ACTIVE

INDICATIVE

Present.

ճանաչեմ, I know. ճանաչես, thou knowest. ճանաչէ, he knows.
ճանաչեմք, we know. ճանաչէք, ye know. ճանաչեն, they know.

Perfect.

ծանեայ, I have known. ծանեար, thou hast known. ծանեաւ, he has known.
ծանեաք, we have known. ծանեայք, ye have known. ծանեան, they have known.

IMPERATIVE

Ճանաչել, to know.

PARTICIPLE

Present.

Ճանաչող, knowing, who knows.

Past.

Ծանուցեալ, having known.

Future.

Ճանաչելոց, who has to know.

PASSIVE

INDICATIVE

Present.

Ճանաչիմ, I am known. Ճանաչիս, thou art known. Ճանաչի, he is known.
Ճանաչիմք, we are known. Ճանաչիք, ye are known. Ճանաչին, they are known.

Perfect.

Ծանուցեալ եղէ, I have been known. Ծա-նուցեալ եղեր, thou hast been known. Ծանուցեալ եղեւ, he has been known.
Ծանուցեալ եղաք, we have been known. Ծանուցեալ եղէք, ye have been known. Ծանուցեալ եղեն, they have been known.

Ճանաչիլ, to be known.

Past.

Ճանուցեալ, known.

This verb is also regular.

NEUTER

INDICATIVE

Present.

Մեղանչեմ, I sin. Մեղանչես, thou sinnest. Մեղանչէ, he sins.
Մեղանչեմք, we sin. Մեղանչէք, ye sin. Մեղանչեն, they sin.

Perfect.

Մեղայ, I have sinned. Մեղար, thou hast sinned. Մեղաւ, he has sinned.
Մեղաք, we have sinned. Մեղայք, ye have sinned. Մեղան, they have sinned.

INFINITIVE

Մեղանչել, to sin.

PARTICIPLE

Present.

Մեղանչող, sinning, who sins.

Past.

Մեղուցեալ, having sinned.

Future.

Մեղանելոց, who has to sin.

This verb is also regular.

NEUTER

INDICATIVE

Present.

Յառնեմ, I rise. յառնես, thou risest. յառ-
նէ, he rises.

Յառնեմք, we rise. յառնէք, ye rise. յառ-
նեն, they rise.

Perfect.

Յարեայ, I have been risen, I rose. յա-
րեար, thou hast been risen. յարեաւ, he
has been risen.

Յարեաք, we have been risen. յարեայք,
ye have been risen. յարեան, they have
been risen.

IMPERATIVE

Արի, rise thou. մի յառներ, rise thou not.
Արիք, rise ye. մի յառնէք, rise ye not.

INFINITIVE

Յառնել, to rise, to get up.

Past.

Թարուցեալ, risen, having been risen.

Future.

Թառնելոց, who is to rise.

ACTIVE

INDICATIVE

Present.

Տամ, I give. տաս, thou givest. տայ, he gives.

Տամք, we give. տայք, ye give. տան, they give.

Perfect.

Եդու, I have given. եդուր, thou hast given. եդ, he has given.

Տուաք, we have given. եդուք, ye have given. եդուն, they have given.

INFINITIVE

Տալ, to give.

PARTICIPLE

Present.

Տուող, giving, who gives.

Past.

Տուեալ, having given.

Future.

Տալոց, who has to give.

PASSIVE

INDICATIVE

Present.

Տուեալ լինիմ, I am given. տուեալ լինիս, thou art given. տուեալ լինի, he is given. Տուեալ լինիմք, we are given. տուեալ լինիք, ye are given. տուեալ լինին, they are given.

Perfect.

Տուայ, I have been given. տուար, thou hast been given. տուաւ, he has been given. Տուաք, we have been given. տուայք, ye have been given. տուան, they have been given.

INFINITIVE

Տուեալ լինել, to be given.

PARTICIPLE

Past.

Տուեալ, given.

Future.

Տալի, which is to be given.

NEUTER

INDICATIVE

Present.

գ.ամ, I come. գաս, thou comest. գայ, he
come th.

գ.ամք, we come. գայք, ye come. գան,
they come.

Perfect.

եկի, I was come. եկիր, thou wast come.
եկն, he was come.

եկաք, we were come. եկիք, ye were come.
եկին, they were come.

INFINITIVE

գ.ալ, to come.

PARTICIPLE

Past.

եկեալ, come, being come.

Future.

գ.ալոց, who is to come.

ACTIVE

INDICATIVE

Present.

ուտեմ, I eat. ուտես, thou eatest. ուտէ,
he eats.

Ուտեմք, we eat. ուտէք, ye eat. ուտէն, they eat.

Perfect.

կերի or կերայ, I have eaten. կերեր, or կերար, thou hast eaten. եկեր, or կերաւ, he has eaten.

կերաք, we have eaten. կերայք, or կերիք, ye have eaten. կերին or կերան, they have eaten.

INFINITIVE

Ուտել, to eat.

PARTICIPLE

Present.

կերող, eating, who eats.

Past.

կերեալ, eating; having eaten.

Future.

Ուտելոց, who has to eat.

PASSIVE

INDICATIVE

Present.

Ուտիմ, I am eaten. ուտիս, thou art eaten. ուտի, he is eaten.

Ուտիմք, we are eaten. ուտիք, ye are eaten. ուտին, they are eaten.

Perfect.

Կերեալ եղէ, I have been eaten. Կերեալ եղեր, thou hast been eaten. Կերեալ եղև, he has been eaten.

Կերեալ եղաք, we have been eaten. Կերեալ եղէք, ye have been eaten. Կերեալ եղեն, they have been eaten.

INFINITIVE

Ուտիլ, to be eaten.

PARTICIPLE

Past.

Կերեալ, eaten.

Future.

Ուտելի or կերլի, which is to be eaten.

ACTIVE

INDICATIVE

Present.

Ըմպեմ, I drink. ըմպես, thou drinkest. ըմպէ, he drinks.

Ըմպեմք, we drink. ըմպէք, ye drink. ըմպեն, they drink.

Perfect.

Արբի, I drank. արբեր, thou drankest. արբ or եարբ, he drank.

Արբաք, we drank. արբիք, ye drank. արբին, they drank.

Ըմպե՛լ, to drink.

Ըմպող, drinking, who drinks.

Past.

Ըմպեալ or Արբեալ, drunk or drunken; having drunk.

Future.

Ըմպելոց, who is to drink.

The passive is formed with a Substantive verb.

Present.

Ունիմ, I take. ունիս, thou takest. ունի, he takes.

Ունիմք, we take. ունիք, ye take. ունին, they take.

Perfect.

Կալայ, I have taken. կալար, thou hast taken. կալաւ, he has taken.

Կալաք, we have taken. կալայք, ye have taken. կալան, they have taken.

INFINITIVE

Ունել, to take, to have.

PARTICIPLE

Present.

Ունող, taking, having, who has.

Past.

Կալեալ, taken, had; taking, having.

Future.

Ունելի or ունելոց, who has to take *or* to have.

NEUTER

INDICATIVE

Present.

Երթամ, I go. Երթաս, thou goest. Երթայ, he goes.

Երթամք, we go, Երթայք, ye go. Երթան, they go.

Perfect.

Գնացի, or չոգայ, I went or I am gone. չոգար, thou wentest or art gone. չոգաւ, he went *or* is gone.

Գնացաք, we went, *etc.* չոգայք, ye went. չոգան, they went or they are gone.

6

INFINITIVE

Երթալ, to go.

PARTICIPLE

Present.

Երթող, going, who goes.

Past.

Երթեալ, gone; going.

Future.

Երթալոց or երթալի, who is to go.

VERBS IMPERSONAL

Those verbs are called Impersonal which are used only in the third person, as,

Ամպէ, it begins to cloud.

Անձրևէ, it rains.

Ցօղէ, it rains little.

Հեղեղատէ, it comes pouring, it runs over.

Ձիւնէ, it snows.

Ճառագայթէ, it shines.

Առաւօտէ, it begins to be day-light.

Մրրկէ, it blows very hard.

Փայլատակէ, it lightens.

Պտղաբերէ, it produces fruit.

Մռնչէ, it bellows, it roars.

Կաղկանձէ, it howls.

Բառաչէ, it bellows, it roars.

Այգանայ, it clears up.

Առաւօտանայ, it dawns.

Երեկոյանայ, it darkens.

Գիշերանայ, it is become night.

Լուսանայ, it brightens.

Խաւարանայ, it grows dusky.

Հրանայ, it kindles.

Որոտայ, it thunders.

Ասի, it is reported, they say.

Երեւի, it appears, it seems.

Թուի, it seems.

Կարծի, 'tis believed, it is thought.

Լսի, it is noised abroad.

Հաստանէ or Հատանի, it happens, it falls out.

Պատահէ, it happens.

Հանդիպի, it happens.

Պիտի, it must, it behoves.

Ցաւէ or ցաւի, it pains.

Անկ է, it becomes, it is fit.

Արժան է, it is convenient, it becomes.

Անհնար է, it is impossible.

Բարւոք է, it is good, it is well.

Խիստ է, it is hard.

Կամ է, or կամք են, it is wished, it wills.

Հարկ է, it must, it is necessary.

Մարթ է, it may be.

Յայտ է, it is clear.

Շատ է, it is enough, it suffices.

Պարտ է, it must.

Վայել է, it is fit, it is proper.

Պէտք են, it must, it is necessary.

Օրէն է or օրէնք են, 'tis lawful, it allows.

Փոյթ է, it is cared for.

Օգուտ է, it is expedient.

'Ի դէպ է, it is suitable, it is convenient, it becomes, it is fit.

PREPOSITION

A preposition is an indeclinable word or particle which placed before a noun changes either it's case, or it's signification.

The prepositions which change the cases of nouns are called *Formers of cases.*

The prepositions which change the meaning of nouns by governing their cases, are called *Rulers of cases.*

Prepositions 'ի, ց, 'ի, ց and — 'ի form the Dative and the Ablative.

Ց, 'ի ց are placed before the vowels.

Ի— forms the Dative.

Ց forms the Dative. Before a consonant it is pronounced ըց, as, ըց+եզ.

Ո forms the Accusative. Before a consonant it was formerly pronounced զց, but at present it is pronounced ըզ.

Ի+զ forms the Dative and the Ablative.

According to the modern usage the Prepositions forming the cases ,, ,, and ց are written prefixed and joined to nouns, and the others detached from them.

A COLLECTION OF PREPOSITIONS

Ա*ռ*, առ 'ի, *to, unto, towards, at: by, near, nigh: for, for the sake, on account: on, upon: under: against: amongst.* govern the dative, the genitive, and the instrumental cases.

Ընդ, *with: by: instead: for: under: between: to, unto, towards: on, upon: amongst.* governs the genitive, the dative, the ablative, and sometimes the instrumental.

Ըստ, *according: for: out: without: after.* governs the genitive, the dative, and the ablative.

Զերդ or զերթ, *as, like.* governs the accusative.

Իբր, իբրև or իբրու, *as, like, about.* govern generally the accusative.

Թարց or թանց, *without, out, unless.* governs the genitive.

Վասն, *for, in order to, concerning.* governs the genitive.

Քան, *than, much.* governs the accusative.

Ինչ see Ընդ.

Մինչ or մինչև, *till, untill, to, unto.* governs the dative with a preposition.

Հանդերձ, *with, by.* governs the instrumental.

Գեր, *over, above, upon, more, before, past.* governs generally the accusative, and sometimes the dative.

6*

Պէս, *as, like,* governs the genitive and the dative.

Գունակ, *as, like.* governs the genitive and the dative.

Դէմ, *towards.* governs the dative.

Կողս or կողմն, *towards.* govern the dative-with-preposition.

Չափ, *till, untill, unto.* governs the instrumental.

Շուրջ, շուրջանակի, *about, around.* govern the circumdative.

Արտաքս, արտաքոյ, *out.* govern the genitive *or* the accusative with չան.

Փոխան, փոխանակ, *instead, inbehalf.* govern the genitive.

Ներքոյ or 'ի ներքոյ, *under.* govern the genitive.

'ի վերայ, *on, upon.* governs the genitive.

'ի վեր, վերոյ or 'ի վերոյ, *over, above.* govern the dative, *or* the accusative with չան.

'ի մէջ or 'ի միջի, *in, into, in the middle, within, between, amongst.* govern the genitive.

'ի միջոյ, *from the middle.* governs the genitive.

'ի ձեռն, *by.* governs the genitive.

Զորէն, *as, like,* governs the genitive.

Զհետ, հետի, զկնի, *after, behind.* govern the genitive.

Յաղագս or աղագաւ, *for, for the sake, because of.* govern the genitive.

'ի *պատճառս* or *պատճառաւ*, *for, for the sake, because, of.* govern the genitive.

'ի *Համար*, *on account, for.* governs the genitive.

Սակս or 'ի *սակս*, *because of, for, on account.* govern the genitive.

'ի *պէտս*, *for.* governs the genitive.

Յաջմէ or *ընդ աջմէ*, *on the right side.* govern the genitive.

'ի *ձախմէ* or *ընդ ձախմէ*, *յահեկէ* or *ընդ աՀեկէ*, *on the left side.* govern the genitive.

Բաց or *բայց*, *out, without, besides, except.* govern the ablative.

Զատ, *aside.* governs the ablative.

Հեռի, *far, far off.* governs the ablative.

Գաղտ, *secretly.* governs the ablative.

Ուրոյն, *apart, aside.* governs the ablative.

Քաւ, *God forbid.* governs the ablative.

Հուպ, *մերձ, մօտ, near, nigh, by.* govern the dative.

Կից, *conjoint, connected, with.* governs the dative.

Զոյգ, *joint, with.* governs the dative.

Նման, *like.* governs the dative.

Հակառակ, *against.* governs the dative.

Փոխարէն, *instead of.* governs the dative.

Առանց, *without, out, besides, unless.* governs the genitive.

Առաջի, *in front, before.* governs the genitive.

Յառաջ, *before, from before.* governs the genitive.

104

Ընդ առաջ, *against.* governs the genitive.

Ընթեր or առընթեր, *near, nigh, by.* govern the genitive and the dative.

Ընդդէմ, *against.* governs the genitive and the dative.

Դէմ ընդդէմ, դէմ յանդիման, Հանդեպ, *in front, against, opposite.* govern the genitive and the dative.

Յանդիման, *before, in front.* governs the genitive and the dative.

Ակն յանդիման or յայտ յանդիման, *before, in front, evidently, publicly.* govern the genitive and the dative.

Մեկուսի, *apart, aside.* governs the ablative.

Յայսկոյս, *on this side.* governs the genitive.

Յայդ կոյս or յայնկոյս, *on that side, beyond, behind.* govern the genitive.

Յառաջ կոյս, *forwards.* governs the genitive.

Յետ կոյս, *back, backward, behind.* governs the genitive.

'ի վեր կոյս, *onward.* governs the genitive.

'ի վայր կոյս, *downward, downwards.* governs the genitive.

Դեպ վերոյ or գեր 'ի վերոյ, *above, higher, over than,* govern the dative and the ablative.

Որպէս, *as, like.* governs generally the accusative.

Դեր քան, 'ի վերոյ քան, գեր 'ի վերոյ քան, *above, higher, over than,* govern the accusative.

Առաւել քան, *over, above, more than.* governs the accusative.

Անդր քան, *beyond, further.* governs the accusative.

Յառաջ քան or նախ քան, *before, first than.* govern the accusative.

Արտաքոյ քան or արտաքս քան, *out than.* govern the accusative.

Յետոյ քան, *after than.* governs the accusative.

Some prepositions are rarely placed after the nouns.

ADVERB

An Adverb denotes the circumstances of a verb, or of an action.

A COLLECTION OF ADVERBS

Այժմ, այժմու, արդ, զարդիս, now, at present, actually, newly, recently.

Այժմէն, already, hence, from this time.

Այսօր or 'ի սերկեանս, 'ի սերկեան աւուր, to-day, in this day.

Վաղիւ, to-morrow.

Երէկ or յերեկն, yesterday.

Երանդ or յերանդն, the day before yesterday.

Ընդ երեկս, in the evening, towards the evening.

Գիշերի, գիշերայն or դգիշերայն, by night, in the night, in the night time.

Զմիջաւուրբ, at noon-day.

Վաղքաշ, early, betimes.

Այգուն or այգուց, in the morning.

Վաղ ուրեմն, վաղու եւս, 'ի վաղուց, alreardy.

Յայսմ՚հետէ or այսուհետե, henceforth, henceforward, hereafter.

Յորմէ՚հետէ, since.

Յետոյ, զկնի, ապա, after, afterwards.

Երբեմն or մերթ, sometimes, now and then, from time to time.

Իրբեւ, երբ, յորժամ, մինչ, when, while, whilst.

Միշտ, յար, յարաժամ, հանապազ, ցանկ, յաւէժ, յաւէտ, always, ever, continually, every moment, evermore, for ever, eternally.

Դեռ, դեռ եւս, տակաւին, yet, still.

Մինչդեռ, այն ինչ, when, while, whilst, as long as.

Մինչե, till, untill.

Չէ, չէ եւս, մինչչեւ, not, not yet, not as yet.

Յայնժամ, then.

Յայնժամ, till then.

Առժամայն, նոյնժամայն, նոյնհետայն, forthwith, very soon, in a moment, immediately, incontinently.

Յանկարծ, յանկարծուստ, յեղակարծ, suddenly, on a sudden, all of a sudden, unawares, in an unexpected manner.

Արագ, երագապէս, փոյթ, soon, as soon
as, quickly, speedily, readily.

Ճեպով, շտապաւ, hastily, in haste.

Հուպ, Հուպընդհուպ, presently, shortly,
by and by, forthwith.

Հազիւ, Հազիւ իմն, scarce, scarcely.

Իսկոյն, իսկ և իսկ, immediately, incontinently, forthwith, instantly.

Անագան, անագան ուրեմն, late, unseason-
ably.

Ուր ուրեմն, scarcely, rarely.

Տակաւ, տակաւ տակաւ, առ սակաւ սակաւ,
by little and little, by degrees.

Աստ or աստանօր, here.

Աստէն, hence; here; in this world.

Աստի, աստուստ, hence, from hence.

Այսր, here.

Այսրէն, here, hitherward; by this way.

Այտի, thence, from thence.

Այդր, այդանօր, there.

Անդ, անդր, անդանօր or անտանօր, there.

Անդէն, thence, there: forthwith.

Անտի, անդուստ, thence, therefrom.

Անդստին, thence, from, since.

Յայս կոյս, on this side.

Յայնկոյս, on that side.

Արտաքս, 'ի դուրս, out, abroad.

'ի ներքս, ներքոյ, within, inwardly.

Հեռի, 'ի բաց, 'ի բացեայ, far, afar, far
off.

'ի բացուստ, 'ի Հեռաստանէ, from afar,
from a great distance.

Մօտ, 'ի մօտոյ, near, nearly, at hand, closely.

Ստորև, 'ի ստորև, 'ի վայր, below, under, hereunder, beneath.

'Ի վեր, 'ի վեր անդր, up, upon, above, hereupon.

'Ի վերուստ, from above.

Ուր, ուրանոր, where.

Ուր ուրեք, where.

Ուստէք, from some place.

Ամենայն ուստէք, from every places.

Յառաջոյ, յառաջ կուսէ, from before.

Յետոյ, after, back, backward, behind.

Յետուստ, յետ կուսէ, 'ի թիկանց, from behind.

Յմ, յոր կոյս, ընդ որ, where, which way.

Այլուր, somewhere else, elsewhere, in another place.

Այլուստ, from elsewhere, from another place.

Միանգամ, առ անգամ մի, առ մի նուագ, once, at one time.

Երկիցս, twice.

Երիցս, thrice.

Չորիցս, four times over.

Հնգիցս, five times over.

Վեցիցս, six times over.

Նախ, նախ առաջին, զառաջինն, first, at first, the first time, in the first place, at the beginning, before.

Երկրորդ, ապա, secondly, after, then.

Մի — միւս, one — another, first — in the second place.

Քանիցս, քանիցս անգամ, how often, how much time, how many times.

Բազում անգամ, յոլովակի, յաճախակի, յոքնակի, oft, often, mostly, many *or* several times, frequently.

Մի ըստ միոջէ, one after another, orderly.

Մի քան զմի, one more than another.

Փոխանակաւ, փոփոխ, by turns, reciprocally, interchangeably, mutually.

Հետ զհետէ, successively, one after another.

Կրկին, կրկնակի, doubly, twice.

Դարձեալ, վերստին, միւսանգամ, անդրէն, again, moreover, once more.

Ի վերջէ or ի վերջոյ, last, lastly, at last.

Ընդէր, զի՞, զմէ՞, հիմ՞, առ ի՞մ, ընդէ՞ր, է՞ր, վասն, վասն է՞ր, յո՞յր սակս, է՞ր ում, առ ի՞նչ, why? wherefore? for why? for what reason?

Զի՞նչ, what? which?

Զիա՞րդ, իՃր, որպէս, how? in what manner? why?

Ո՞չ, ո՞չ ապաքէն, is it not?

Քանի՞ն, how much?

Ի՞ւ, ի՞ւ իւիք, by which? how?

Մի՞, մի՞թէ — եթէ՞, or — either?

Ուստի՞, from whence?

Ե՞րբ, յո՞րժամ, when?

Այո՛, yes.

Արդարև, յիրավի, հաւաստեաւ, իսկապէս,

անշուշտ, truly, verily, certainly, surely, indeed, in truth, assuredly, infallibly, undoubtedly, justly, really.

կարի քաշ, very well.

Ապաքէն, արդեօք, truly, verily.

Գրեթէ, գմգ, գոգցես, almost, nearly, as it were, pretty near.

Օն և ձն, so, thus.

Գուցէ, գուցէ թէ, գուցէ երբէք, թերևս, արդեօք, իցէ թէ, իցէ զի, perhaps, lest, it may be.

Միթէ, մի՛ արդեօք, may it be.

Ո, ոչ, no, not.

Եւ ոչ, nor, neither.

Ո՛չ ևս, no more.

Ո՛չ բնաւ, ամենևին ոչ never, by no means.

Ոչ ինչ, nothing.

Այլ ոչ ևս, no more.

Մի, մի՛ բնաւ, մի՛ երբէք, մի՛ ցցէ, մի՛ ինչ, no, not, never, by no means.

Օն անդր, forbear.

Քաւ, God forbid, forbear.

Միայն, եւեթ, լոկ, սոսկ, only, but.

Միայնակ, միայն ընդ միայն, singly, solely.

Մի, մի, one by one.

Մեկուսի, ուրոյն, առանձինն, առանձնակի, apart, aside, asunder, separately, singly, particularly.

ԱՀա, behold, lo, see, there.

ԱՀաւասիկ or *աւասիկ*, behold, here.

ԱՀաւադիկ or *աւադիկ*, behold, there.

ԱՀաւանիկ or *աւանիկ*, there behold.

Նամ, մանաւանդ, նա մանաւանդ, այն զի, յաւէտ, առաւել, տի, տինա, rather, more, than, nay, chiefly.

Ինձէն, by my-self.

Քեզէն, by thy-self.

Մեզէն, by our-selves.

Զեզէն, by your-selves.

Այժմէն, from since, from this time.

Ինքնին, by himself.

Գլխովին, almost, quite, totally.

Բոլորովին or բոլորովիմբ, wholly, totally, entirely.

Կամաւ or կամովին, voluntarily, willingly.

Երբէք, ever, at any time.

Ուրէք, in some place.

Ուստի, whence, from whence.

Յարի, too, much, most, too much.

Իւրովի, by himself.

Ձրի, freely, for nothing, gratis.

Ուժգնակի, violently, vehemently.

Կողմնակի, side-ways, obliquely.

Ուղղակի, directly, perpendicularly, in a straight line.

Զեռամբացի, with or by hand.

Նշանացի, with a sign.

Աքացի, by or with kicking.

Հայերէն or Հայեցի, in Armenian.

Եբրայեցերէն, in Hebrew.

Հրեարէն, in the Jewish language.

Յունարէն, in Greek.

Կենդանւոյն, alive.

Ազգովիմբ, nationally, with whole family.

112

Ամէնեւիմբ, wholly, totally.

Դիւրաւ or Հեշտեաւ, easily, readily, without trouble, at leisure.

Իննաւ, totally, almost, ever.

Խստիւ, severely, cruelly, rudely, hardly.

Կանխաւ, before, beforetime, formerly.

Ճշդիւ, exactly, sparingly.

Ճշմարտիւ, truly, indeed, really, certainly.

Մեղմով, softly, gently, slowly, mildly, quietly, peaceably.

Բարւոք or բարւոքապէս, well, rightly.

Ի բնէ, naturally, by nature, radically, originally.

Յառաջնմէ or յառաջուց, before, already, primitively, formerly.

Ի մասնէ, partly, in part.

Յոյժ, too, much, too much, very much, most.

Յարժանի, worthily, justly.

Առաւօտու or առաւօտուց, in the morning.

Յանչափս, exceedingly, excessively, immoderately, extremely.

Մարդկօրէն, մարդկաբար, մարդկապէս, humanly, as a man.

Արտաքուստ, from without, outwardly.

Յայնմ հետէ, thenceforth, thenceforward.

Նոյնչափի, so much, so many.

Միանգամայն, at once, together.

Ի Հարեւանցի, superficially, carelessly.

Արագ արագ, fast, hastily, quickly, speedily, soon.

Որպէս, as, how.

Որզան, որբար, որպէս, as.

Համօրէն, totally, wholly, altogether.

Ընդ վայր, in vain, needless, to no purpose.

Այլընդայլո, diversly, otherwise, contrarily.

Ընդ ամենայն, altogether, totally, wholly.

Եւս քան զեւս, more and more.

Այսպէս, սոյնպէս, so, in this manner.

Այդպէս, դոյնպէս, so, thus in that manner.

Այնպէս, նոյնպէս, thus, in that manner.

Նմանապէս, in like manner, so, thus.

Նոյնորինակ, alike, so, thus.

Միորինակ, alike, equally, in the same manner.

Զիարդ, որպէս զիարդ, as, like how.

Զորօրինակ, as, for example.

Զարաչար, badly, sadly, ill, miserably, cruelly.

Այլապէս, այլազգապար, diversly, otherwise.

Յայտնի, յայտնապէս, evidently, clearly, openly, publicly.

Մեկին, մեկնորէն, explicitly, plainly, openly, clearly.

Լու 'ի լու, publicly, openly.

Ծածուկ, 'ի ծածուկ, ծածկապար, գանլխապար, secretly, in secret, under hand.

Լռելեայն, լռիկ ինն, silently, tacitly, quietly.

Դիւրապար, easily.

Բռնի, բռնապար, forcibly, by force, violently.

Դժուարաւ, hardly, not easily, scarcely.

Ի հարկէ, հարկաւ, necessarily, inevitably.

Յակամայս, unwillingly, forcibly, with regret.

Կամնկար, 'ի կամակարուց, willingly, voluntarily, readily.

Զուր, 'ի զուր, տարապարտուց, վայրապար, ընդ վայր, 'ի նանիր, in vain, vainly, to no purpose, without any reason.

Յանդէպս, unfitly, improperly, amiss, absurdly.

Յանգէտս, ignorantly, unknowingly.

Նենգաւ, by fraud, fraudulently, deceitfully.

Ի մերկուց, nakedly.

Հետի, Հետիոտս, on foot.

Նորոգ, newly, recently, freshly, lately, just now.

Այսչափ, այսքան, so much, so many.

Այդչափ, այդքան, so much, so many.

Որչափ, որքան, as much, how much, how many, as far.

Համանգամայն, միանգամայն, 'ի միասին, առ հասարակ, together, altogether, all at once, wholly, totally, completely, entirely, in the mean while.

Շատ, much, many, greatly, a great deal, very, enough.

Յաւէտ, առաւել, more, at most, too much, very much.

Առաւել քան, more than.

Սակաւ, սակաւ մի, սակաւիկ ինչ, խուն մի, խուն ինչ, փոքր մի, դոյն ինչ, փոքր 'ի չատէ, little, but little, some, somewhat, something, less, in a small quantity.

Բաւականապէս, sufficiently, well enough, duly, tolerably.

CONJUNCTION

A Conjunction is an indeclinable word which connects the parts of speech together, or one sense with another.

A COLLECTION OF CONJUNCTIONS

Եւ, եւ or ու, and, or.

Եա, եւս ե, ե եւս, այլ, այլեւ, նաեւ, նաեւս, իսկ, դարձեալ, also, too, still, yet, more, even.

կամ, եւ կամ, կամ թէ, թէ, եթէ, or, either.

Այլ, բայց, սակայն, համայն, այլ սակայն, բայց սակայն, բայց միայն, բայց եթէ, միայն, միայն թէ, քան թէ, եթէ ոչ, but, only, unless, except, save, nevertheless, notwithstanding, however, yet, provided, upon condition that, if not.

Թէ եւ, թէեպէտ, թէեպէտու, though, although, however.

Թէեւ ոչ, though not.

Ո՛չ եթէ, իբր ոչ եթէ, no, not.

Ո՛չ միայն, not only.

Ա՛յս է, այն է, նա՛ է, այսինքն, այսինքն է, it is, that is to say, to wit.

Որպէս, իբր, իբրև թէ, որպէս այն թէ, իբր այն թէ, as, if it were.

Ըստ որում, as, how.

Օրինակ իմն, զօրօրինակ, as, for example.

Արդ, և արդ, այլ արդ, բայց արդ, իսկ արդ, ապաքէն, then, therefore, in consequence, now.

Այն զի, rather.

Զի, քանզի, վասն զի, որպէս զի, փոխանակ զի, այնու զի, այն զի, նա զի, որովհետև, մինչ, for, because, that, whereas, forasmuchas, in order to, to the end that, since.

Ուր, where.

Որ, that.

Ապա, ուրեմն, ապաքէն, ապա ուրեմն, նա ուրեմն, ուստի, վասն որոյ, այսր աղագաւ, ամէն իրի, զմէն իրի, նմէն իրի, այսու հետևութ, then, therefore, wherefore, in *or* by consequence, for this reason.

Քան, քան թէ, առաւել, մանաւանդ, յաւէտ, նա, թող, թէ, than, rather, at most, on the contrary.

Մինչ, մինչև, մինչզի, անդ ամ, զի, զի և, so that, till, untill.

Թէ, եթէ, իսկ թէ, ապա թէ, ապա եթէ or **ապե թէ**, if.

Ապա թէ ոչ, otherwise.

Գէթ, գոնէ, գոնեայ, at least.

Թէ, եթէ, և թէ, զի, բայ, բամ, որ, that.

INTERJECTION

An Interjection expresses the passions of
the soul.

A COLLECTION OF INTERJECTIONS

երանի, երանի թէ, յանկարծ, իցէ թէ,
իցիւ, ոլ, օչ, would to God, may it be!

Ո՛, ոլ, ոլ թէ, բաբէ, վա՛չ, oh! oh! won-
derful! see! o God!

Ո՛ ո, ոլ, ոՀ, ոՀ ոՀ, էՀ, լՀ, վայ, վայ վայ,
ալ ալ, ափսոս, աղէտ, աւաղ, եղուկ, բաբէ,
oh! alas! woe be to! poor! wretch that!

վա՛չ, վա՛չ վա՛չ, ոՀ ոՀ, oh joy!

վա՛Հ, վա՛չ, ոՀ, յէՀ, էՀէ, Հէ, Հը, այ, է,
a! ah!

Ա՛յ, ոլ, իշտ, այի, o! fie! pish!

Ա՛ղէ, Հապա, օն, Հա՛, come, come on,
cheer, well well.

Թող, forbear.

Ա՛ծ, բեր, bring, come.

Ե՛կ, եկ բեր, come, come bring.

SYNTAX

Syntax is the due conjunction or con-
nexion of the parts of speech.

Substantives agree with each other in
three ways.

1. When another substantive is added to
express and explain the former more fully,
as, Կղէոպատրա դաւերն հանդերձ. with
Cleopatra his *daughter.* Եւ զԿղէոպատրա ըզ-
դուստր իւր. he has given *Cleopatra* his
daughter. Երթէլ ՚ընդդարբրն իւրովք, որ-
դւքն Իսրայելի. to visit his *brethren the
children* of Israel.

2. When one thing is said to belong to
another, as, Գիրք ծննդեան Յիսուսի Քրիս-
տոսի` որդւոյ Դաւթի` որդւոյ Աբրահամու.
the book *of the generation of* Jesus Christ,
the son *of David,* the son *of Abraam.* Հային
վկայութիւն առաքեալքն յարութեանն Տեառն
gave the apostles witness *of the resurrection
of the Lord.*

3. When a substantive or gerund like a
verb governs another substantive, as, Յետ
ընդունելութեան գիտութեան ճշմարտութեանն.
after that *we have received the knowledge* of
the truth. Յղատմեռութէն ուսուցանես ՚ի Մով-
սէս` որոյ ՚ի Հեթանոսս ամենայն Հրէայք

Են. thou teachest all the Jews which are among the Gentiles *to forsake Moses.* Բայց ղՀոգւոյն Հայհոյութեն մի՛ Թողցի. but the *blasphemy against the (Holy) Ghost* shall not be forgiven.

Substantives agree with Adjectives when governed by the same, as, Մեզ Սարակարարք լմնեին նոցին՝ որք այժմ պատմեցան. unto us *they did minister the things,* which are now reported. Չծնողս անարգուք. disobedient to parents. Եղէգն շարժուն 'ի Հողմոյ. a reed *shaken with the wind.* Գեղեցիկ 'ի տեսանել, և քաղցր 'ի կերակուր. that is pleasant to the sight, and good for food. Եւ 'ի կանանց գլխաւորաց ոչ սակաւ. and *of the chief women* not a few. Եւնես կոյր մի 'ի ծնէ. he saw a man which was *blind from his birth.* Եւ Աբրամ էր մեծատուն յոյժ անասնով, և արծաթով, և ոսկւով. and Abram was very *rich in cattle, in silver,* and *in gold.* Բայց Ռաքէլ էրէր տեսեանէ, և գեղեցիկ երեսօք. but Rachel was *beautiful* and *well-favored.* Ողջամիտս 'ի Հաւատս, 'ի սէր, 'ի Համբերութեան. sound in faith, in charity, in patience. Եւ մեծն 'ի ձեզ՝ եղիցի ձեր սպասաւոր. but he that is *greatest among you* shall be your servant. Արատերագոյն յորդիս նորա. *the youngest of* his *sons.*
The Comparatives govern generally the Accusative with the preposition քան, as, Զի

կարի *դորատրակոյն* *ջան* *դեղ* *եղեր.* for thou
art much *mightier than we.* *Մեծ* *ջան* *զՅոն*
նա *է* *աստ.* a greater than Jonas is here.

Also the Middle nouns govern different
cases, as, Ահա Ադամ եղև իբրև զմի 'ի մէնջ.
behold, the man (Adam) is become as *one
of us.* Ո՞չ սրբեսցէ զանձն իւր 'ի կանանցա_
ծնայ. how can he be clean *that is born of a
woman?* Եւ ոչ Տէրի իսկ է յհրապատանէս ու_
ձէք 'ի մէնջ. though he be not far *from every
one of us.* Ո այլ ոչ յԱռաքելոց անրէ ոչ տեսի.
but *other of the Apostles* saw I none.

CONCORDANCE OF ADJECTIVES WITH

SUBSTANTIVES

1. The adjective may be placed before
or after the substantive; joined, or divided
from it.

2. The adjective may or may not be of the
same case or number with the substantive.

3. The governing preposition may be
placed either before the substantive or adjective, or before both being repeated.

Examples.

Սեդդանէ և Ճշմաշենական բանէն Աստուծոյ.
by *the word of God, which liveth* and *abideth
of ever.* Մեծման և կատարելոյն և անձեռա_
գործ խորանաևն. by *a greater* and *more per-*

122

fect tabernacle, not made with hands. 'ի վե
րայ ձեռոյ պարանոցէ նորա. upon *the smooth of
his neck*. Եքեցէս զմիս նորա 'ի սրբումն տե
ղւոջ. seethe his flesh *in the holy place*. Վասն
ամենայն եղելոց զօրութեանդ. for *all the mighty works*. Դարձան յԵրուսաղէմ յանուա
նեալ լեառնէն Ձիթենեաց. returned they unto
Jerusalem *from the mount called Olivet*. Եւ
մեծամեծս եւս քան զդոսա ցուցանէ նմա գործս.
and he will shew him *greater works* than
these. Եւ պատմեաց Աստուած զփարա
ւունս պարծօ մեծամեծօ եւ չարօ եւ զտունն նո
րա. and the Lord plagued Pharaoh and his
house *with great plagues*. Կէսկէզզիքեան աւե
լորդա ճաչելով ծածկեսցես զապարումն փեղ
կից խորանին յետոյ կողմանէ. the *half-curtain that remaineth*, shall hang over the backside of the tabernacle. Որ եւ լսիցեն զանուա
նէ յասմէ մեծէ, եւ զձեռանէ յասմէ հզորէ, եւ
զբազկէ յասմէ յկելոյ. for they shall hear *of
thy great name, and of thy strong hand*, and
of *thy stretched-out arm*. Եկն կին մի որ ու
նէր շիշ եւղոյ նարդեան՝ պատուի մեծագնոյ. there
came a woman having an alabaster-box *of
ointment of spikenard, very precious*. Տեսի
զՏէր նստեալ յաթոռ բարձրութեան եւ վե
րացելոյ. I saw also the Lord sitting *upon a
throne, high and lifted up*. Տէր, զազգ մի
զանկեա եւ զարդար կորուսանիցես. Lord, wilt
thou slay also a *righteous nation* ? 'ի Հարդոյ
մեղաւորէ նենգաւորէ փրկեա զիս. o deliver me
from the deceitful and unjust man. Բայց վե

դու մարդկան ոչ ոք կարէ Հնազանդել՝ զչարն
և դանկադ և չլի Թունօք մաՀաբերին. but
the tongue can no man tame : *it is an unruly
evil, full* of deadly poison. Յուսմունս պէս_
պէսս և յօտարաձայնս. with divers and
strange doctrines. Առ Հարսն եղեյ ա-ե-
տեայն. *of the promise made unto our fathers.*
'Ի բերանոյ երկ--ց և երից վկայից Հասատատես_
ցի ամենայն բան. in the mouth *of two* or
three witnesses every word may be esta_
blished. Նոյ էր ամաց վեցՀարերոց. Noah was
six hundred years old. իբրև ասպարիսոյ Հնկե_
տասան. about *fifteen furlongs off.* 'ի վեցՀա_
րիւրորդի և 'ի միում ամի ,յամենանն առաջ_
նում: in the six hundredth and first year,
in the first month. Իշէ՞ք գնոց զդեսօրն վա_
ձառեցիք. և նա ասէ, այդ այդչափ. whether
ye sold the land *for so much ?* and she said,
yea, *for so much.* Այր այսպիսի. such a
one as this is. Զի դոյ--թ-ն+ այտապիտ+ 'ի
ձեռաց սորա լինիցին. that even *such mighty
works* are wrought by his hands. Յորէ՞ ա-
էարԿէ ես, կամ յորմէ՞ ժողովրդեէ. what is
thy country? and *of what people* art thou?
Որււ դատաստանա- դատիք.whith what judge-
ment ye judge. Ո՞րն է-ա է իմ, կամ զ՞ն
յանցանք են իմ. what is my *trespass, what* is
my *sin*? Համդերձ ձերո-վ ամակ+, և ձարտա_
բխոս- Տերտ-ղ-ա- ամակ. with *the elders,
and* with *a certain orator* named *Tertulus.*
Եգիտ Հրեայ դ-ն անուն Ակիղաս. and
found *a certain Jew* named Aquila. 'ի Հո_

վս̃ե ﬕոջէ. from one shepherd. *Օ բ̃ն ﬔ̅ ﬔ̅ առ քեզ Հաստուանիցեն, և դ̅*տ*ք ﬔ̅ ꝗ̅ ֊ պատան ﬕնքեանք դատեսցեն.* Every great *matter* they shall bring unto thee : but *every small matter* they shall judge. *Ն̃ա՝ աւանիկ տղ֊ա֊հ̃անի էն ցանկայեալ էն, այս ինքն է՝ երկն̄ա֊որքն.* but now they desire *a* better country, that is, *an heavenly.* Առանց երկբ̄ ֆ̃ղ̅ելոյ. doubting nothing. *Ի գալ ﬕ֊ոյ շաբաթուն.* the next sabbath (or sabbath-day.) *Ա̃յլոյք բանիւք բազմօք.* with many other words. *Առ այլ երնꝗ̅քե.* by the other kine. *Ի դառնալ ﬔ̅ զ*ꝗ̄*տ̅անꝗ̅ե֊ր ի ꞩ̅ արեաց ﬕ̅րոց.* in turning away every one of you from his iniquities. *Ի վերայ ﬕոյ ուրուք ի ﬔ̅րանց.* upon some mountain.

Notwithstanding the great licence in the use of adjectives the following rules must be generally observed.

1. The adjective placed after the substantive must agree with it in number and case, as, *քարամբք ﬔ̅ծ֊ա֊ﬔ̅ծօք,* with great stones. *զօրութիւնք այսպիսիք,* such mighty works.

2. The adjective placed before a substantive does not agree with it, excepting the monosyllable adjectives, as, *ﬔ̅ծ֊ա֊ﬔ̅ծ քա֊ րամբք,* with great stones. *այսպիսի զօրու֊ թիւնք,* such mighty works. *այլոյք բանիւք,*

with other words. 'ի սրբում տեղւոջ, in the holy place.

3. When a verb or participle is before the substantive and after the adjective, the adjective agrees readily with the substantive, as, աստուածային զինէ զօրութեամբ, he armeth with divine force. աստուածային զի֊ նեալ զօրութեամբ, armed with divine force.

4. An adjective with the article or the letter distinctive of the person, placed before a substantive, agrees with it in number and in case, but not always, as, մեծաւն և կա֊ տարելովն և անձեռագործ խորանաւն, by a greater and more perfect tabernacle, not made with hands.

5. When there are many substantives before one adjective only, the adjective is in the plural, and agrees with them, as, Սա֊ ւուղ և Յովնաթան սիրելիք և գեղեցիկք և վայելուչք, Saul and Jonathan (were) lovely and pleasant.

6. The governing preposition is joined to the case which precedes it, whether substantive or adjective, as, յանուանեալ լե֊ ռնէն, from the mount called. 'ի մարդոյ մե֊ ղաւորէ նենգաւորէ, from the deceitful and unjust man.

7. When the adjectives or substantives placed before are joined with the conjunction և, and, the governing preposition is applied to all, as, յանեղծ և յանարատ և յանթա֊ ռամ ժառանգութիւնն, to an inheritance

126

incorruptible, and undefiled, and that fadeth not away. 'ի Հնազանդութիւն և 'ի Հեղումն արեանն, *unto obedience and sprinkling of the blood.*

8. When the adjective or substantive placed before is simple, and many substantives or adjectives follow, the governing preposition governs the first word, and the second and third which follow; however not always, as, 'ի չար խորհրդոց, 'ի բանից և 'ի գործոց, *from evil thoughts, words, and works.* զայր արիւնահեղ և զնենգաւոր, *the bloody and deceitful man.*

CONCORDANCE OF PRONOUNS

The personal pronouns Ես, *I,* դու, *thou,* ինքն, *he* or *himself,* are substantives, and as substantives agree with adjectives, as, վասն ձեր կեղծաւորաց, *of you hypocrites.*

Ինքն signifies sometimes *self,* as, ես ինքն մարդ եմ. *I myself also am a man.*

The definitive pronouns սա, դա, նա, *he (she, it)* are substantives, and so agree with adjectives, as, Դոքա յետինքերդ. *these last.* Եւ կամ ինքեանք սոքա ասասցեն. *or else let these same here say.*

The definitive pronouns սոյն, դոյն, նոյն, *this, that, same,* are adjectives, and so agree with substantives, as, 'ի սոյն or 'ի սմին աւուր. *on this day, or in the course of this day,* or to-day. *Ըստ դմին օրինակի.* in the like manner. *'Ի նմին զանգուածոյ.* of the same lump. *Յորդգայթ 'ի նոյն անկցի.* into that very destruction let him fall. *Եւ սմին այսմիկ զամենայն փոյթ 'ի միջ առեալ.* and besides this, giving all diligence.

The definitive pronouns *այս*, this, *այդ*, *այն*, that, are generally adjectives, but sometimes substantives, as, *Զի՞նչ գործեցեր զայդ.* what is this that thou hast done? *Այս են ծնունդք որդւոյն Նոյի.* these are the generations of the sons of Noah. *Յայս երկուս պատուիրանս.* on these two commandments. *Որոց զայս ինդ միմեանս երդմունս արարեալ էր.* who had made this conspiracy. *Եթէ եղեալ իցէ ըստ բանիս մեծի այսորիկ.* whether there hath been any such thing as this great thing is? *'Ի չարեացդ քոց յայդցանէ.* of this thy wickedness. *Թղթովդ այդուիկ.* by this epistle. *Ըստ ամենայն բանիցս այսոցիկ, եւ ըստ ամենայն տեսլեանս այսորիկ.* according to all these words, and according to all this vision. *Երանի որ պահէ զբանս մարգարէութեանս զայս.* blessed is he that keepeth the sayings of the prophecy. *Յազգէ յայդմանէ.* of this generation. *Անձինք ծառայից քոց այսոցիկ յիսնից.* the life of these fifty thy servants. *Կեցցե՞մ 'ի հիւանդութենէ աստի իմմէ յայսմանէ.* shall I recover of this disease? *Զայս Մովսէս՝ զոր ուրացանն... զնա Աստուած իշխան եւ փրկիչ առաքեաց.* this Moses, whom they re-

fused... the same did God send to be a ruler and a deliverer.

The possessive pronouns *իմ*, my, *քո*, thy, *մեր*, our, *ձեր*, your, *իւր*, his, his own, are adjectives. When they are without substantives, receive either the articles *ս*, *դ*, *ն*, or the adverbs *սոյն*, *նոյն*, as, *իմ է ամենայն ինչ, և 'ի քոյոցդ տուաք քեզ.* all things come of thee, and thine own have we given thee. *Հանգեաւ յիւրոց գործոց անտի, որպէս և Աստուած յիւրայոցն.* he also hath ceased from his own works, as God did from his.

The pronouns possessive derived *իմային* or *իմոյին*, my, *ձերային* or *ձերոյին*, your's, are put before the substantives.

The pronoun relative *որ*, who, which, what, that, is substantive, and in different manners agrees with antecedent and following nouns, as, *Աչս՝ որովք ոչ տեսանիցեն, և ականջս՝ որովք ոչ լսիցեն*, Eyes that they should not see, and ears that they should not hear. *Լուաւ 'ի նմանէ վասն որ 'ի Քրիստոս Յիսուս հաւատոյն*, heard him concerning the faith in Christ. *Զի մի ինչ եկեսցէ 'ի վերայ իմ յորոց դուք ասէք*, that none of these things which ye have spoken come upon me. *Որում խնդրէ 'ի քէն՝ տուր, և որ կամի փոխ առնուլ 'ի քէն՝ մի դարձուցանէր զերեսս*, give to him that asketh thee, and from him that would borrow of thee turn not thou away. *'Ի վախճան աւուրցս այսոցիկ խօսեցաւ ընդ մեզ որդւովն, զոր եդ ժառանգ*

ամենայնի, որով և զյաւիտեանսն արար, որ
է լոյս փառաց, hath in these last days spok-
en unto us by his son, whom he hath appoint-
ed heir of all things, by whom also he made
the worlds. Who being the brightness of his
glory. *Եւ պատմեաց Մովսէս Ահարոնի զա_*
մենայն պատգամսն՝ զոր առաքեաց զնա Տէր,
and Moses told Aaron all the words of the
Lord who had sent him. *Եւ ամենայն արք*
տանն նորա՝ ընտոծիկք և արծաթագինք՝ որ
էին յաղգաց օտարաց, թլփատեաց զնոսա,
and all the men of his house, born in the
house, and bought with money of the stran-
ger, were circumcised with him. *Յորոց դուն*
՚ի խնդիր երթեալ էիր, which thou wentest
to seek. *Որոց զարիւնն Պիղատոս խառնեաց*
ընդ զոհսն նոցա, whose blood Pilate had
mingled with their sacrifices. *Առ որ մատու_*
ցեալ ՚ի վէմն կենդանի, to whom coming, as
unto a living stone. *Որոյ սերմն իւր ՚ի նմին,*
whose seed is in itself. *Եւ ժողովեցին, որ*
շատ, և որ սակաւ, and gathered, some more,
some less.

The articles-distinctive-of the persons *ս*
of the first, *դ* of the second, *ն* of the third,
besides showing the persons joined to the
terminations of words, have also the force
of the English articles *a* and *the*, and give
energy and ornament, as, *Տէր և Վարդա_*
պետ (without any article) Lord and Master,
but with the article *ս* so, *Տէրս և Վարդա_*
պետս, it may have three senses: 1°. I who

am a Lord and a Master. 2°. *This Lord and Master*. 3°. *My Lord and Master*. So Տէրդ Լ վարդապետդ, 1°. *Thou who art a Lord and a Master*. 2°. *That Lord and Master*. 3°. *Thy Lord and Master*. Likewise Տէրն Լ վարդապետն, 1°. *His Lord and Master*. 2°. *That Lord and Master*. 3°. *The Lord and the Master*. Զօր զՀետ եկեալ էս Արքայդ Իսրայէլի, *after whom is the King of Israel come out*? Տեղիս անապատ է, Լ օրս տարա֊ ժամեալ, *this is a desert place, and the time is now past*. Զի՞նչ իրք էն՝ վասն որոյ Լ կիքդ, *what is the cause wherefore ye are come*? Եթէ ընդ փայտ դալար զայս առնեն, ընդ չորն զի՞նչ լինիցի, *if they do these things in a green tree, what shall be done in the dry*? Ա՛ռ դու զորդիդ քո սիրելի, զոր սիրեցեր դԻսահակ, *take now thy son, thine only son Isaac, whom thou lovest*. Արտաքին մարդս մեր, *our outward man*. Զի՞նչ իցէ ՚ի մեռե֊ լոյն յառնել, *what the rising from the dead should mean*? Մեկնեցարուք ՚ի վրանաց ա֊ րանց խստասրտացդ այդոցիկ, *depart (I pray you) from the tents of these wicked men*. Յա֊ րանցս յայսցանէ եկելոցս ընդ մեզ, *of these men who have companied with us*. Ո՞վ արար զխուլս Լ զՀամի, զականս Լ զկոյր, *who maketh the dumb, or deaf, or the seeing, or the blind*? Եկայք ՚ի Հարսանիս, *come unto the marriage*. Յոր եդդ իշանեմ, *in the midst whereof I dwell*. Յերիցունէ առ Գայիոս սի֊ րելի, զոր եդդ սիրեմ Ճշմարտութեամբ, *the *elder unto the well-beloved Gaius, vhom I love in the truth.* Զի ուր եմն իջեմ, և դուք անդ իջէք, *that where I am, there ye may be also.* Զոր դուդ առնես, *that thou doest.* Որում դուն վկայեցեր, *to whom thou bearest witness.* Մինչ առ ձեզս եմ, *being yet present with you.* Զոր նայն առնէ , *what things soever he doeth.* Զոր սայս առնէ, *which this man hath done.* Տեսանիցէք զոր ընտրեացդ իւր Տէր, զի ոչ դոյ նմանն դորա յա֊մենեցին 'ի ձեզ, *see ye him whom the Lord hath chosen, that there is none like him among all the people.* Ո'վ է որ ասէդ զքեզ, *who it is that saith to thee.* Ընդ որում և Համարձակեալդ խօսիմ, *before whom also I speak freely.* Զիշխանաց աշխարՀիս այսորիկ ըզխափանելեացս, *of the princes of this world that come to nought.* Զիայրդ այժմ տեսա֊նէ, *but by what means he now seeth.* Որպէս և կանխաւն ասէի, *as I have also told you in time past.* Իսկ յոր ոչն իջէն սորա մերձ, կոյր է և զայացու, *but he that lacketh these things is blind, and cannot see afar off.*

CONCORDANCE OF VERB

The verb which is not a participle, or infinitive, is governed by a nominative, as, Իսկզբանէ արար Աստուած զերկինս և զեր֊կիր, *in the beginning God created the heaven and the earth.* Եւ երկիր էր անեղիոյթ և աներպատրաստ, and the earth was without form, and void. Եւ Հոգի Աստուծոյ շրջէր 'ի վերայ Ջուրց, and the Spirit of God moved upon the face of the waters.

The participle and the infinitive are often governed by a genitive, as, Նախ ծնանին, մինչչեւ է մտեալ առ նոսա մանկաբարձաց, they are delivered ere the midwives come in unto them. Բանալ երկնից, եւ իջանել Հոգւոյն սրբոյ... եւ գալ ձայն յերկնից, the heaven was opened, and the Holy Ghost descended.... and a voice came from heaven.

In like manner are governed the preter-perfect, and the preter-plu-perfect tenses formed by a participle, and a substantive verb, as, Եւ ոչ գիտէր Յակովբ՝ թէ Ռաքէլայ կնոջ իւրոյ գողացեալ էր զնոսա, for Jacob knew not that Rachel had stolen them. Դարձան գործեալ է եմ 'ի նոցանէ առանց աւելի քան զքառասուն, there lie in wait for him of them more than forty men.

The accusative cannot properly govern a verb, but is subject to it, as, Եւ արդ որովկ Հետն աղգ եմք Աստուծոյ, ոչ պարտիմք Համարիլ ոսկւոյ՝ կամ արծաթոյ՝ կամ քարի, որ 'ի Ճարտարութենէ եւ 'ի մտաց մարդկան քանդակեալ իցէ՝ զաստուածականն լինել նմանող, forasmuch then as we are the offspring of God, we ought not to think that the Godhead is like unto gold, or silver, or stone, graven by art and man's device.

The nominative of nouns agrees gene-

rally in number with a verb which is not a
participle or infinitive, excepting those without singular number, or collective, as, Յարեաւ այլ ազգ, որ ոչ ճանաչէին զՏէր, there
arose another generation after them, which
knew not the Lord. Եկն ժիաբան բազմու-
թիւնն, եւ խռնեցաւ, զի լսէին յիւրաբան-
չիւր լեզուս խօսել նոցա, the multitude came
together, and were confounded because that
every man heard then speak in his own language. Եւ ժողովուրդն անն ունէր Զաքա-
րիայ, եւ զարմանային ընդ յամէին նորա, and
the people waited for Zacharias, and mar-
velled that he tarried so long.

The nouns joined with the conjunction եւ,
and sometimes agree, sometimes not, as, Եւ
մեծացաւ այրն յոյժ յոյժ, եւ եղեւ նորա ոչխար եւ արջառ յոյժ, ծառայք եւ աղախնայք,
ուղտք եւ էշք, and the man increased exceedingly, and had much cattle, and maid-ser-
vants, and men-servants, and camels, and
asses. Եզէն իմ արջառ եւ ոչխար եւ էշք, ծառայք եւ աղախնայք, I have oxen, and asses, flocks, and men-servants, and women-
servants.

When the noun or, pronoun is only one,
the verb must be of the same person, as, Ես
միայն մնացեալ էի, եւ սորա ուր էին, I was
left alone ; where had they been?

When the persons are different the verb
agrees with the first, as, Դալով գայցէք
ես եւ մայր քո եւ եղբարք քո, եւ երկիրպա-

զանիցե՞մք քեզ, shall I, *and thy mother and thy brethren, indeed come to bow down our-selves to thee to the earth?* Յորժամ դու և նա միայն իցէք, *between thee and him alone.* Եթէ ես, և եթէ նոքա այսպէս քարոզե-ցաք, *whether it were I or they, so we preach.*

Sometimes the verb is supposed, as, Մեք կաւ, և դու ստեղծիչ մեր, և գործք ձե-ռաց քոց ամենեքին մեք, *we are the clay, and thou our Potter; and we all are the work of thy hand.*

The verb active governs generally the ac-cusative, as, Եւ արար Աստուած զմարդն 'ի պատկեր իւր․ րստ պատկերի Աստուծոյ արար զնա․ արու և էգ արար զնոսա, *so God created man in his own image; in the image of God created he him; male and fe-male created he them.* Եւ տնկեաց Աստուած զդրախտն յեդեմ ընդ արևելս, և եդ անդ զմարդն զոր ստեղծ, *and the Lord God plant-ed a garden eastward in Eden; and there he put the man whom he had formed.*

Sometimes the letter զ a sign of the ac-cusative is supposed, as, Նա տայ ամենայնի կեանս և շունչ, և զամենայն ինչ, *he giveth to all, life, and breath, and all things.* Եւ առ մի 'ի կողից նորա, և եղից ընդ այնր մար-մին, *and he took one of his ribs, and closed up the flesh instead thereof.*

The verb active governs secondly another accusative, as, Դու զի՞ առնես զքեզ, *whom makest thou thyself?* Թագաւոր զմի ասեն *զՅիսուս*, *saying that there is another king, one Jesus.*

The verbs active as well as the neuter and passive govern often their roots in the accusative, as, Սէր յաւիտենական սիրեցի զքեզ, *I have loved thee with an everlasting love.* Ամաչեսցեն զամօթ մեծ, *they shall be greatly ashamed.*

The verb passive governs generally the ablative, as, Զի լցցի որ ասացան 'ի Տեառնէ, *that it might be fulfilled which was spoken of the Lord.* Քանզի 'ի պտղոյ անտի ծառն Ճանաչի, *for the tree is known by his fruit.* Ճանաչեմ զիմոն, և Ճանաչիմ յիմոցն, *I know my (sheep) and am known of mine.*

The infinitive sometimes is noun, and sometimes verb.

The preposition '*ի* put before an infinitive has often the signification of an adverb յորժամ, զի, *when as,* 'Ի տեսանելըն զքեզ, քերկրեսցի 'ի միտս իւր, *when he seeth thee, he will be glad in his heart.*

The infinitive or the gerund with its verb increases the signification of it, as, Ունել ունէր պարծանս, *he hath whereof to glory.* Միթէ Թագաւորելով Թագաւորեսցես, 'ի վերայ մեր, կամ տիրելով տիրեսցես մեզ, *shalt thou indeed reign over us? or shalt thou indeed have dominion over us?*

CONCORDANCE OF PREPOSITIONS.

Prepositions sometimes are put after the nouns; they change their places, and are re-doubled, as, Ոյք հաւետալ էին յԱստուծոյ իրաւանցն վերայ, *who knowing the judge-ment of God.* Մի ինչ պատճառս տալ հակա-ռակորդին 'ի Հայհոյութեան ապագս, *give none occasion to the adversary to speak re-proachfully.* Զհետ երթային բազումք 'ի Հրէից անտի, և 'ի պաշտօնէիցն եկամոքյ զՊաւղոսի և զԲառնաբայ *many of the Jews and religious proselytes followed Paul and Barnabas.* Յամենայն ժամ զբարեաց զհետ երթայք, *but ever follow that which is good.* Յորժամ 'ի պէսպէս փորձութեանց 'ի մէջ անկանիցիք, *when ye fall into divers tempta-tions.* Հատուցին ինձ չար փոխանակ ընդ բարւոյ, *that render evil for good.*

Adjectives are often used as adverbs, as, Մեծաձայն կարդացէք, *cry aloud.* Երագս ընթանային, և թեթեւս դառնային, *they ran and returned.*

On the contrary sometimes adverbs are used as adjectives, as, Եղև նորա ոչխար և արջառ յոյժ, *and had much cattle.*

Negative adverbs -չ, չ and մի, *no, not,* sometimes are put after verbs, as, Եւ խոզ՝ զի թաթահերձ է, և կճղակս ունի, և որո-ճայ ոչ՝ պիղծ իցէ նա ձեզ, *and the swine, though he divide the hoof, and be cloven-*

footed, yet ye cheweth not the cud: he is
unclean to you.

ACCENTS, OR NOTES OF PROSODY

1°. Շեշտ or շեշտանշան (´) as, ծառ,
բաց, Ես, Ճանապէ, անդ, բայց, մէ, մի, մի,
գլ'Նս ։

2°. Բուխ or բխանշան (`) as, նախ, երկ-
րորդ` դարձեալ` արդ` այնդի` այլ` ։

3°. Պարույկ or ոլորակ (°) as, մի, գիարդ,
ուր ։ According to modern usage it is em-
ployed as an interrogative point, and as a
note of admiration.

4°. Երկար (´), as, բամէ, վաչ, նրուսաղէմ նրուսաղէմ ։

5°. Սուղ (°) as, Շ'Նազանդ, բ'Նուխիւն,
Ս'րոխէ ։ It is put on the syllable to make
it short.

6°. Թաւ (ˆ) as, թիւ, թուˆոց ։ It is put
by some moderns upon the letter ւ to mark
its pronunciation as a վ ։

7°. Ապախարց (ˈ). It is rarely used.

8°. ԵՆխամնայ, the mark of division of a
word (‿).

PUNCTUATION

There are three Points in the Armenian.

1°. Ստորակէտ (,)
2°. Միջակէտ (.)
3°. Վերջակէտ (:)

8*

138

OTHER MARKS

1°. Մակակէտ (') . It is put on the head
of the letter ի, when it forms a preposition,
as, 'ի, առ'ի:

2°. Պատիւ (՟) mark of abbreviation, as,
Ած (Աստուած). Այ (Աստուծոյ). Քս
(Քրիստոս). Քսի (Քրիստոսի). Տր (Տէր).
Տն (Տեառն):

3°. Սինն (,) which is one of the three
columns of a ա entire; it is put sometimes
to mark an entire ա, as, աշտրիկ (աշտա-
րակ), պարրիկ (պարարակ):

4°. Երկոտեակ (") which marks the vowels omitted, or the words shortened, as,
ք"զ"ք (քազաք): Յովմ". (Յովհաննէս):

5°. Փակագիծ ().

6°. Պատուագիր. The sign, or substitute
of a word, as, ☞ (աշխարհ):

7°. Փակագիր, Cyper.

The letters of the Armenian Alphabet are used as the Numbers, generally with a line on the letter, so

ա ,	1.	*ճ* ,	100.
բ ,	2.	*մ* ,	200.
գ ,	3.	*յ* ,	300.
դ ,	4.	*ն* ,	400.
ե ,	5.	*շ* ,	500.
զ ,	6.	*ո* ,	600.
է ,	7.	*չ* ,	700.
ը ,	8.	*պ* ,	800.
թ ,	9.	*ջ* ,	900.
ժ ,	10.	*ռ* ,	1000.
ի ,	20.	*ս* ,	2000.
լ ,	30.	*վ* ,	3000.
խ ,	40.	*տ* ,	4000.
ծ ,	50.	*ր* ,	5000.
կ ,	60.	*ց* ,	6000.
հ ,	70.	*ւ* ,	7000.
ձ ,	80.	*փ* ,	8000.
ղ	90.	*ք* ,	9000.

NB. ○ and ֆ being recent letters, are not included in the numeration.

VERSE

The antient Armenian Verses or Songs were not rhymed, as the following for example.

Երկներ երկին և երկիր, երկներ և ծիրանի ծով.

Երկն'ի ծովուն ունէր զկարմրիկ եղեգնիկն.

Ընդ եղեգան փող քոց ելանէր,

Եւ 'ի քոցոյն պատանեկիկ վազէր.

Նա հուր հեր ունէր.

Ապա թէ քոց ունէր մօրուս,

Եւ աչկունքն էին արեգակունք։

But now they are rhymed generally and are composed from five Syllables to fifteen. The following few lines are specimens with their own translation in prose.

of 5 Syllables.

Սէր անուն Յիսուս
Սիրով քով Յշմեամ
Սիրտ իմ քարեղէն։

Jesus, whose name is a love, bind thou my heart of stone with thy love.

of 6 Syllables.

Եղեալ Հարսն անմահ՜ին ,
Երկնաւոր Փեսային :

Having been the bride of the immortal
celestial Bridegroom.

of 7 Syllables.

Արիաբար դու մրցեա
'Ի Հանդիսի բստատին :

Valiantly fight thou in the public combat.

of 8 Syllables.

Սիրեա զուսումն որով պատուիս
'Ի յերկնայնոց և 'ի յերկրիս :

Love thou instruction, by which thou
wilt obtain honor from Heaven, and on
earth.

of 9 Syllables.

իկաՃեմ աղաւնի օդապար ,
Նոր Նոյեան տապանն է քոյդ դադար :

Thou dove, ever flying through the air,
the Ark of the new Noah is thy dwelling.

of 10 Syllables.

Այսօր երևի անտեսն 'ի բարձանց,
Բանին դպրութիւնք քոյր եղականք ։

To-day the Invisible appears from on
high; the knowledge of all creatures is dis-
covered.

of 11 Syllables.

Բանաւոր ծառոց երևեցան ծաղիկք,
նրբնապարդ գունով, անուշահոտ քուր-
մամբ ։

Flowers of rational Plants appeared of
various tints, and delicious odour.

of 12 Syllables.

Բոլորակ եմ կիսագունտ որպէս խորան,
Բնութեամբ կայուն, անձամբ շարժուն,
անտեսական ։

I am a hemisphere round as a pavilion,
by nature firm, in reality moveable invisibly.

of 13 Syllables.

Դոյումն որատման յետ Հոսելոյն դանձրև
կենաց,

Ս.միտւիեալ յերկինս, առ Ս.րաբողն մեզ_
բէն դարձաւ ։

The roar of thunder having diffused the
rain of life, is recovered to the heavens,
returning to his Origin.

of 14 Syllables.

Բանիւ աւետաւոր բարանւաբալ բարբա_
ռեցուք
Առքեղ եկեղեցի, դուստըր վերինըն Սիովնի ։

Let us cry aloud in joyful tidings address-
ing thee personally, O Church, daughter
of lofty Sion.

of 15 Syllables.

Որ 'ի վերայ ջուրցն գոլով ստեղծանէիր
զարարածս,
Իջեալ 'ի ջուրս Աւազանին, ծնանիս որդիս
Աստուծոյ ։

Thou, who brooding on the waters didst
make creation, descending in the waters of
the Baptismal fount, dost give birth to the
Sons of God.

www.ingramcontent.com/pod-product-compliance
Lightning Source LLC
Chambersburg PA
CBHW030558270326
41927CB00007B/979